HE CALLS, WE ANSWER

St. Josemaría Escrivá on Vocation

HE CALLS, WE ANSWER

St. Josemaría Escrivá on Vocation

BORJA DE LEÓN

Scepter

Published by Scepter Publishers, Inc.

info@scepterpublishers.org

www.scepterpublishers.org

800-322-8773

New York

All rights reserved.

Cover and text by Studio Red Design

Cover Image: Photo by Mark Tegethoff, Unsplash.com

Library of Congress Control Number: 2021937656

Paperback: 9781594174223

eBook: 9781594174230

Printed in the United States of America

Table of Contents

PREFACE

During the month of October 2018, the ordinary general assembly of the Synod of Bishops took place in Rome, which Pope Francis had wanted to be about "Young People, the Faith and Vocational Discernment." In the letter he wrote to young people announcing this event, the Holy Father evoked the encounter of the first disciples with our Lord: "Jesus looks at you and invites you to go with him. Dear young people, have you noticed this look towards you? Have you heard this voice? Have you felt this urge to undertake this journey?"

The personal encounter with Jesus can be difficult to achieve today, with "the noise and confusion seemingly prevalent in the world." Nevertheless, "[his] call continues to resonate in the depths of your heart so as to open it to joy in its fullness." It will be possible to achieve this, the Pope says, with "professional guides" from whom "you will learn how to undertake a journey of discernment to discover God's plan in your life." The following series of articles seeks to assist young people on this journey. Guided by Jesus' first disciples, by the teachings of the pope, the saints, and St. Josemaría, we can move more deeply into this perennial reality: God is calling us. "He has a plan for each person: sanctity."[1]

St. Josemaría recalled how at the age of sixteen he discovered that his heart was asking *for something great, and that it was love.*[2] May we, too, discover and rediscover this—because love is always new, always surprising, always great.

---

1   From an address by Mons. Fernando Ocáriz in Argentina on August 5, 2018.
2   Andrés Vázquez de Prada, *The Founder of Opus Dei*, vol. 1 (New York: Scepter, 2001), p. 86.

INTRODUCTION

The Gospels are full of personal encounters with Jesus: John and Andrew; Peter; Matthew; Martha, Mary and Lazarus; Nicodemus; the Samaritan woman. These stories are much more than a memory of the past. They are episodes in a story that is still happening and is still full of action, even today. Although it may seem difficult to meet Jesus in the midst of the rush and hectic activity around us, in fact his call continues to resonate in the hearts of young people. It is what makes them, in the depths of their hearts, to continue wanting big things. "They want injustice to stop. They want inequalities to be overcome and everyone to participate in the goods of the earth. They want the oppressed to be free. They want big things. They want good things."[1] That is why we Christians continue to announce, in the midst of the twenty-first century, that God cares a great deal about us, that he wants us to be happy, and that he is counting on us to make his love the force that moves the world.

1   Pope Benedict XVI, Address to the German Pilgrims Who Had Come to Rome for the Inauguration Ceremony of the Pontificate (April 25, 2005). Vatican website: www.vatican.va.

"Who am I?" is an important question. But much more important, Pope Francis tells us, is this one: *"For whom* am I?"[2] Our identity is rooted in what we have received, but it takes its form above all from the love to which we dedicate our life. Loving God, letting ourselves be loved by him, giving his love to others—thus do we discover who we are. The series of articles in this book, written by priests who work with young people, are geared to help us to make this discovery. With the first disciples of Jesus, with the teachings of the popes, of the saints, of St. Josemaría, we can move more deeply into this perennial reality: God calls us; he has a plan for each one of us, and that plan is holiness.

The book has three sections. The first section includes three articles that present, within a broad framework, the reality of God's call and the encounter with him. The second section is longer: it presents different vocational paths and dwells on some aspects of the discernment of our own vocation. The final section is addressed to those who have already been following our Lord for some years; it is an invitation to contemplate, with grateful memory, the beauty of a life following Christ.

St. Josemaría recalled how, when he was only sixteen years old, he discovered that his heart was asking him for "something great,

---

2   Pope Francis, Post-Synodal Apostolic Exhortation to Young People *Christus Vivit* (March 25, 2019), 286. Vatican website: www.vatican.va.

and that it was love.[3]" May we also discover and rediscover, because love is always young, always surprising, always great.

Borja de León | Priest, Doctor in Philosophy. He carries out his pastoral work with families and is chaplain in a school in Madrid.

PART I
THE
ENCOUNTER

CHAPTER 1

JESUS COMES TO MEET US

Borja Armada

The next day again John was standing with two of his disciples; and he looked at Jesus as he walked, and said, "Behold, the Lamb of God!" The two disciples heard him say this, and they followed Jesus. Jesus turned, and saw them following, and said to them, "What do you seek?" And they said to him, "Rabbi" (which means Teacher), "where are you staying?" He said to them, "Come and see." They came and saw where he was staying; and they stayed with him that day, for it was about the tenth hour. (Jn 1:35–39)

Those taking part in this Gospel scene must have spoken about it with deep emotion, for it marked the most important moment in their life: the day on which they encountered, for the first time, Jesus of Nazareth.

Meeting Christ is truly the decisive experience for every Christian. As Benedict XVI forcefully said at the beginning of his pontificate: "Being Christian is not the result of an ethical choice or a lofty idea, but the encounter with an event, a person, which gives life a new horizon and a decisive direction."[1] It is also quite significant that Pope Francis reminded us right from the start: "I invite all Christians, everywhere, at this very moment, to a renewed personal encounter with Jesus Christ, or at least an openness to letting him encounter them; I ask all of you to do this unfailingly each day."[2] We want to renew this invitation here, following in the footsteps of the youngest apostle, St. John.

Who is Christ for me? Who am I for him?

The fourth Gospel uses a wonderful phrase to capture the identity of the youthful John: he was "the disciple whom Jesus loved." Nothing more needed to be said: John was someone Jesus loved. Over the years this conviction never paled, but rather grew ever stronger: "In this is love, not that we loved God but that he loved us" (1 Jn 4:10). This certainty in our Lord's love for him is surely what enabled him to maintain, right to the end of his life, a deep and contagious joy—the same joy that we sense in his Gospel. Everything began that day, on the banks of the Jordan.

---

1   Pope Benedict XVI, Encyclical on Christian Love *Deus Caritas Est* (December 25, 2005), 1.

2   Pope Francis, Apostolic Exhortation on the Proclamation of the Gospel *Evangelii Gaudium* (November 24, 2013), 3.

And in our case, have we too experienced such a heartfelt encounter as the young apostle's? Even if we have been Christians our whole life and have spent many years praying, it is good to stop to consider: Who is Christ for me? What does Christ mean in my real life, today? Thus can we take stock of our faith. "But before asking this question, there is another question that is inseparable and prior to it, and that in a certain sense is more important: Who am I for Christ?"[3]

In raising these questions, it is only natural that we find ourselves a bit perplexed. Who am I for Christ? Who am I? A tiny insignificant creature? A product of evolution? Just another human being who has to fulfill Christ's commandments? How does Jesus see me? We can draw light here from looking at the saints. Once, when St. John Paul II was asked a similar question, he answered: "*You are a thought of God, you are a heart-beat of God.* To say this is like saying that you have a value which in a sense is infinite, that *you matter to God in your completely unique individuality.*"[4] What he himself had discovered—what all the saints have discovered—is how much we matter to God. We aren't insignificant creatures, servants who are only in the world to do what he wants. We are truly friends. Everything that is ours matters to him, and therefore he is concerned about us and accompanies us throughout our entire life, although often we fail to realize it.

3   Notes taken at a family gathering with Msgr. Ocáriz. General Archives of the Opus Dei Prelature, Library, P03, 2017, p. 146.

4   St. John Paul II, Address to Young People from Kazakhstan (September 23, 2001).

All this is no exaggeration. Jesus himself told his apostles: "Greater love has no man than this, that a man lay down his life for his friends. You are my friends…. I have called you friends, for all that I have heard from my Father I have made known to you (Jn 15:13–15). These words are still very relevant today. Jesus "is alive and saying it to you now. Listen to his voice with great openness; he has something to say to each one."[5] Who am I, then, for Christ? I am a friend, whom he loves with the greatest love. I am a beat of his heart. That's who I am for him. And he, who is he for me?

May You Seek Christ!

On May 29, 1933, a young architecture student spoke with St. Josemaría for the first time. His name was Ricardo Fernández Vallespín. Many years later he recalled:

> The Father talked to me about what was going on in my soul…. He gave me some advice and encouraged me to be better. I remember perfectly, with a vivid memory, that before bidding me good-bye, he got up and went to a bookcase and picked up a book he was using. And on the first page, as a dedication, he wrote these three phrases: *May you seek Christ! May you find Christ! May you love Christ!*[6]

---

5   Pope Benedict XVI, General Audience (August 2, 2006).

6   St. Josemaría Escrivá, ed. Pedro Rodríguez, *The Way: A Critical-historical Edition* (New York: Scepter, 2009), commentary on no. 382.

The apostle John set out to seek Christ, even without knowing exactly whom he was seeking. But he knew he was looking for something that would fill his heart. He hungered for a fulfilled life. He wanted more out of life than only to work, to earn money, to be like everyone else. His heart was restless, and he wanted to quiet this restlessness. Therefore, he followed the Baptist. And it was while he was with him that Jesus passed by his side. The Baptist pointed him out: "Behold, the Lamb of God!" And he and his friend Andrew "heard him say this, and they followed Jesus" (Jn 1:36–37).

What can we do to follow in the footsteps of the young apostle? First, listen to our restless heart. Give heed to it when it isn't satisfied, when a worldly life fails to fill it, when it wants more than earthly goods and satisfactions. And then draw close to Jesus. In fact, perhaps in a certain sense this is easier for us than it was for John. Many people have already pointed out to us where Jesus can be found: *Usually we learn to invoke God as a young child from our Christian parents. Later, teachers, friends and acquaintances have helped us in many ways not to lose sight of our Lord.*[7] Therefore what we need to do now is to seek him: *Seek him then, hungrily; seek him within yourselves with all your strength. If you act with determination, I am ready to guarantee that you have already found him, and have begun to get to know him and to love him, and to hold your conversation in Heaven.*[8]

---

7   St. Josemaría Escriva, *Christ is Passing By* (New York: Scepter, 2002), 1.
8   St. Josemaría Escriva, *Friends of God* (New York: Scepter, 1996), 300.

May You Find Christ!

When John and Andrew began to follow Jesus that first time, they must have found themselves a bit embarrassed. How should they introduce themselves to him? They couldn't just go up and ask him, "Are you the Lamb of God?" But that was what the Baptist had told them, and it was all they really knew about him. Perhaps they were debating among themselves what they should do, when Jesus himself "turned, and saw them following, and said to them, 'What do you seek?'" (Jn 1:38).

Our Lord is moved by young, restless hearts. So, when we seek him sincerely, he himself comes to meet us in the most unexpected way. St. Josemaría remembered his first personal and unexpected encounter with Jesus all his life. He was only an adolescent, with his heart filled with plans and ideals. After a night of heavy snow, he left home in the morning, only to discover, with surprise, the footprints left by the sandals of a discalced friar in the snow. He followed the trail and spoke with the friar. This experience left a deep impression on his soul: *If others can make such sacrifices for God and neighbor, can't I offer him something?*[9]

That day, like John and Andrew, the youthful Josemaría followed in the footsteps of our Lord, who now made himself present in some *footprints in the snow*. Many other people probably saw those prints, but for that young boy they were an unmistakable sign that Jesus wanted to enter into his life. And his reaction was very similar

9   Andrés Vázquez de Prada, *The Founder of Opus Dei*, vol. 1, p. 85.

to those first friends of Jesus: "[T]hey said to him, 'Rabbi' (which means Teacher), 'where are you staying?' He said to them, 'Come and see.' They came and saw where he was staying; and they stayed with him that day, for it was about the tenth hour (Jn 1:38–39).

Discovering that someone loves us as a great friend awakens in us a hunger to get to know that person. Discovering that someone is concerned about us, that someone is waiting for our response and has the answer for our deepest longings spurs us to seek that person. Those footprints had a deep effect on the heart of St. Josemaría: "He now had, very deep inside, 'a divine restlessness' that moved him to a more intense life of piety."[10]

But seeking Jesus and finding him is only the beginning. We can then begin to draw close to him as a friend. We can strive to get to know him better by reading the Gospels, going to Mass, enjoying intimacy with him in Communion, caring for him in those most in need. And we can make ourselves known to him, sharing with our friend our joys and sorrows, our plans and failures. Because after all, this is what prayer is: "drawing close to him in friendship, often spending time alone with the Person who we know loves us."[11] Like John and Andrew, who spent that entire day with Jesus.

10   Andrés Vázquez de Prada, *The Founder of Opus Dei*, vol. 1, p. 85.
11   St. Teresa of Ávila, *The Book of Her Life*, 8, 2.

May You Love Christ!

For the youthful John, the day he found Jesus was the day his life changed. Of course, he still had a long way to travel. Alongside Jesus he would experience the miraculous catch of fish and the journeys through Palestine; the words that brought joy to people's hearts and the miracles; the affectionate care for the sick, the poor, the outcasts; but above all, those hours of conversation alone with the Master—the dialogue that began one afternoon, next to the river Jordan, and that would last his entire life.

We have all experienced how deeply a friendship can change us. That is why parents need to be watchful concerning the friends their children make. Without even realizing it, our relationships with our friends transform us little by little, leading us to love what they love and reject what they reject. Friendship unites so deeply that two friends can be said to share "one and the same soul that sustains two bodies."[12]

In this sense, it is striking to see the transformation in the life of the young apostle. He and his brother James were called the "sons of thunder" (Mk 3:17), and several incidents in the Gospels show us that this wasn't an excessive term. Two examples are the time when some Samaritans refused to welcome Jesus and his disciples to their village, and when the two brothers asked the Master: "Lord, do you want us to bid fire come down from heaven and consume them?" (Lk 9:54). Nevertheless, little by little, as their friendship with our

12   St. Gregory Nazianzen, *Sermon 43.*

Lord grew, they learned to love as Jesus did, to understand others as Jesus did, and to forgive as Jesus forgave.

The same can happen to each one of us. Encountering Jesus and getting to know him will lead us to want to love as he loves. We shouldn't be surprised to see our heart being consumed with this desire; rather we should be filled with gratitude, because our Lord wants to count on us to make his love present in the world. That is what happened to St. Josemaría. Those footprints in the snow gave him the deep conviction that he had a mission to carry out on this earth. *I began to have intimations of Love, to realize that my heart was asking for something great, and that it was love.*[13] We too need to discover, behind these calls of our heart, the echo of the voice of Jesus that we often hear in the Gospels: *Follow me!*

Living Our Entire Life with Christ

Looking back on his life, John saw how much had depended on the opportunity to follow Jesus. That is how God acts in each person: "The surpassing love of Jesus impelleth to great works, and exciteth to the continual desiring of greater perfection. Love willeth to be raised up, and not to be held down by any mean thing."[14] That is what happened to John, to Peter, to James, to Paul, to Bartimaeus, to Mary Magdalene, and to so many other people since Jesus came into the world. Our Lord's presence in the world is no less real today

---

13   Andrés Vázquez de Prada, *The Founder of Opus Dei*, vol. 1, p. 86.
14   Thomas à Kempis, *The Imitation of Christ*, bk. 3, chap. 5.

than it was back then. In fact, Jesus is even more present now, since he can live in each one of us. More than inviting us to share in the mission he has received from his Father, Jesus wants to love with our life, with the heart of each one of us. "Abide in my love," he tells us (Jn 15:9), in order to reconcile this world with him, to transform hate into love, selfishness into service, rancor into forgiveness.

The youthful apostle, who had discovered the love of our Lord, accompanied him right to the Cross. Later, with the rest of the apostles, he received a mission that would shape his entire life: "Go into all the world and preach the gospel to the whole creation" (Mk 16:15). We too, if we listen to our restless heart and follow Jesus, if we find him and follow him, if we are his friends, will discover that he is relying on us. He will ask us to help him, each in our own way, in the Church—as a friend who, since he loves us, asks us to take part in an inspiring endeavor. "Today Jesus, who is the way, the truth and the life, is calling you, you, and you to leave your mark on history. He, who is life, is asking each of you to leave a mark that brings life to your own history and that of many others. He, who is truth, is asking you to abandon the paths of rejection, division and emptiness. Are you up to this?"[15]

15   Pope Francis, Prayer Vigil with Young People during World Youth Day in Krakow (July 30, 2016).

CHAPTER 2

WHAT OUR LIVES COULD BE

Nicolás Alvarez de las Asturias

Mesopotamia saw the rise and fall of some of the world's oldest civilizations: Sumerians, Babylonians, Chaldeans. Although we might study them in school, these cultures seem distant and irrelevant to us today. And yet this geographical landscape was the home of a person who forms a part of our own family. His name was Abram, until God changed his name to Abraham. The Bible says he lived 1,850 years before the birth of Christ. Four thousand years later we still remember him, especially at Mass when we invoke him as "our father in faith,"[1] because he began our family.

---

1   *Roman Missal*, Eucharistic Prayer I.

I Have Called You by Name

Abraham is one of the first people to go down in history for responding to God's call. In his case, the request was a very special one:
"Go from your country and your kindred and your father's house
to the land that I will show you" (Gen 12:1). After him came others:
Moses, Samuel, Elias, and the other prophets. All of them heard
God's voice inviting them in one way or another to "go forth" from
their land and begin a new life in his presence. As with Abraham,
God promised each of them that they would do great things in
their lives: "I will make of you a great nation, and I will bless you,
and make your name great, so that you will be a blessing" (Gen
12:2). Furthermore, he called each of them *by their name*; therefore,
besides recounting God's actions, the Old Testament includes the
names of those who have responded to God's call. The letter to the
Hebrews showers them with praise (chapter 11).

When God sent his Son into the world, the dynamic of his
calling changed. Those called not only heard God's voice; they also
saw a human face: Jesus of Nazareth. God called them too to begin
a new life, and to leave an indelible mark on history. And we know
their names: Mary Magdalene, Peter, John, Andrew, and the rest.
And we also remember them with gratitude.

And then what? It might seem that, with Jesus' ascension into
heaven, God retires from human history. But not only does he
continue acting: his action increases. During his passage on earth
he chose only a small group of people. But in the last two thousand

years God has "changed the plans" of thousands upon thousands of men and women, opening up new horizons that they themselves would never have imagined. We know the names of many of them, for they have been inscribed by the Church as saints. Then there is an immense multitude of men and women "from all tribes and peoples and tongues" (Rev 7:9), unknown saints who are the real "protagonist[s] of history."[2]

Today, at this very moment, God continues to seek and knock at the door of every person. St. Josemaría liked to consider this text from the prophet Isaiah: "I have redeemed you; I have called you by name, you are mine" (Is 43:1). He said that for him meditating on these words was *as sweet as honey from the comb*,[3] because they made his heart sense how much God loved him, in a personal, unique way.

These words can be like honey from the comb for us as well, because they show us how important our life is for God. He counts on every person, and invites each man and woman to follow him. The dream of all Christians is to have their name written on God's heart; and this dream is within everyone's reach by responding to his call.

"Look Up at the Sky and Count the Stars, If You Can"

It might seem excessive to look at our lives in this way, as a continuation of the lives of the great saints. We have experienced our

2   Pope Francis, Prayer Vigil with Young People during World Youth Day in Krakow (July 30, 2016).

3   St. Josemaría Escriva, *Friends of God*, 312.

own weakness. So did Moses, Jeremiah, and Elijah, who all had bad moments.[4] Isaiah himself, for example, once said: "I have labored in vain, I have spent my strength for nothing and vanity" (Is 49:4). It is true that sometimes life can feel like this to us, like something without meaning or interest, on seeing how easily our efforts are cut short. The question, "What am I living for?" seems to come to shipwreck on experiencing failure, suffering, and death.

God knows perfectly our weakness, and how disconcerted we can be by it. Nevertheless he seeks us out. The prophet doesn't let himself give in to cries of complaint but recognizes the voice of the Lord: "I will give you as a light to the nations, that my salvation may reach to the end of the earth" (Is 49:6). We are weak, but this isn't the whole truth about our life. As the pope wrote: "Let us acknowledge our weakness, but allow Jesus to lay hold of it and send us too on mission. We are weak, yet we hold a treasure that can enlarge us and make those who receive it better and happier."[5]

The divine call is a great mercy of God: a sign that he loves me and that I matter to him. "God counts on you for what you are, not for what you possess. In his eyes the clothes you wear or the

---

4   See, for example: "I am not able to carry all this people alone, the burden is too heavy for me. If thou wilt deal thus with me, kill me at once, if I find favor in thy sight, that I may not see my wretchedness" (Num 11:14–15); and, "Why did I come forth from the womb to see toil and sorrow, and spend my days in shame?" (Jer 20:18); and also, "It is enough; now, O Lord, take away my life; for I am no better than my fathers" (1 Kgs 19:4).

5   Pope Francis, Apostolic Exhortation on the Call to Holiness *Gaudete et Exsultate* (March 19, 2018), 131.

kind of cell phone you use are of absolutely no concern. He doesn't care whether you are stylish or not; he cares about you, just as you are! In his eyes, you are precious, and your value is inestimable."[6] With his call, God frees us. He allows us to escape from a petty life dedicated to small satisfactions that can never quench our thirst for love. *When we make up our minds to tell our Lord, "I put my freedom in your hands," we find ourselves loosed from the many chains that were binding us to insignificant things, ridiculous cares, or petty ambitions.*[7] God frees our freedom from its pettiness, opening it up to the great horizon of his love, where each man and woman is a protagonist.

Our calling discloses to us the meaning of our existence. It means being convinced, through faith, of the reason for our life on earth. Our life, the present, past, and future, acquires a new dimension, a depth we did not perceive before. All happenings and events now fall within their true perspective: we understand where God is leading us, and we feel ourselves borne along by this task entrusted to us.[8] For those who hear and respond to God's call, no deed is small or insignificant. Everything in our life is ennobled by the promise, "I will make of you a great nation" (Gen 12:2): with your life I will do great things; you will make an impact; you will be happy by spreading happiness. Therefore "when He asks us for something, in reality He is offering

6   Pope Francis, Homily at Closing of World Youth Day, Krakow, July 31, 2016.
7   St. Josemaría, *Friends of God*, 38.
8   St. Josemaría, *Christ is Passing By*, 45.

us a gift. We are not the ones doing Him a favor. It is God who illuminates our life, filling it with meaning."[9]

At the same time, the light of a vocation allows us to understand that the importance of our life isn't to be measured by the *human* grandeur of the things that we do. Only a small handful of people get their names included among history's great figures. However, *divine* grandeur is measured by our relation to the only plan that is truly great: the Redemption. "Certainly the most decisive turning points in world history are co-determined by souls whom no history book ever mentions. And we will only find out about those souls to whom we owe the decisive turning points in our personal lives on the day when all that is hidden is revealed."[10]

The Redemption is taking place—now![11] How can I help to further it? In a thousand different ways, knowing that God himself will give us light to help us discover the specific way of assisting him. "God wants the person's freedom to intervene not only in the response, but also in the shaping of each one's vocation."[12] And the person's response, while still free, is also prompted by actual graces sent by God. If we begin walking, starting from wherever we find ourselves, God will help us see what he has dreamed for our life. It

9   Msgr. Fernando Ocáriz, "Light to See, Strength to Want To," September 24, 2018. Available at opusdei.org.

10   St. Teresa Benedicta of the Cross (Edith Stein), *Verborgenes Leben und Epiphanie*: GW XI, 145.

11   St. Josemaría, *The Way of the Cross*, Station 5, 2.

12   Msgr. Fernando Ocáriz, "Vocation to Opus Dei as a Vocation in the Church," in *Opus Dei in the Church* pp. 99–146 (New York: Scepter, 2003).

is a dream that "takes clearer shape" as we go forward, because it also depends on our own initiative and creativity. St. Josemaría said that if we dream, our dreams would fall short, because those who truly dream, dream with God. And God encouraged Abraham to "dream big": "Look toward heaven, and number the stars, if you are able." (Gen 15:5).

Shared between Two

God enters Abraham's life to stay, uniting himself in some way to Abraham's destiny: "I will bless those who bless you, and him who curses you I will curse; and by you all the families of the earth shall bless themselves" (Gen 12:3). Abraham's story is one of "shared protagonists." It is the history of Abraham *and God*, of God *and Abraham*. So much so, that from this moment on, God presents himself to other men and women as "the God of Abraham."[13]

The call consists, above all, in living with him. More than doing special things, it means trying to do everything with God, doing *everything for Love!*[14] The same thing happened to the first disciples. Jesus chose them, above all, "to be with him"; only afterwards, the evangelist adds, "to be sent out to preach" (Mk 3:14). Therefore, we too, when we hear God's voice, shouldn't view it as a "mission impossible," something that is extremely difficult, imposed from on high. If it is a true calling from God, it will be an invitation to

---

13   See Ex 3:6 and Mt 22:32.
14   St. Josemaría, *Intimate Notes*, 296, September 22, 1931 (cited in *The Way: A Critical-historical Edition*, commentary on no. 813).

enter into his life, his plan; an invitation to abide in his love (Jn 15:7). And thus, from God's heart, from an authentic friendship with Jesus, we can bring his love to the whole world. He wants to rely on us, while being with us. Or rather, he wants to be with us, while relying on us.

Hence, we can see why those who experience God's call and follow him seek to encourage those who in turn are beginning to sense his call. Often, they may at first feel afraid. This is only natural in the face of something unexpected, the unknown, a much broader horizon, the reality of God seeking us, which can at first overwhelm us. But this fear is not meant to last; it is a very common human reaction and shouldn't surprise us. It would be wrong to let ourselves be paralyzed by it: rather, we need to face our fear, finding the courage to analyze it calmly. Great decisions in life, projects that leave a lasting impact, have almost always been preceded by fear, which is overcome by calm reflection—and yes, by a good dose of courage too.

St. John Paul II began his pontificate with an invitation that still rings out today: "Open the doors to Christ.… Do not be afraid!"[15] Benedict XVI referred back to these words upon his election, pointing out that "the Pope was speaking to everyone, especially the young." And he himself asked,

> Are we not perhaps all afraid in some way? If we let Christ
> enter fully into our lives, if we open ourselves totally to

15   St. John Paul II, Homily at the Beginning of His Pontificate (October 22, 1978).

him, are we not afraid that He might take something away from us? Are we not perhaps afraid to give up something significant, something unique, something that makes life so beautiful? Do we not then risk ending up diminished and deprived of our freedom?[16]

And Benedict XVI continued:

The Holy Father wanted to assure us: No! If we let Christ into our lives, we lose nothing, nothing, absolutely nothing of what makes life free, beautiful and great. No! Only in this friendship are the doors of life opened wide. Only in this friendship is the great potential of human existence truly revealed. Only in this friendship do we experience beauty and liberation.[17]

Uniting himself to that advice of St. John Paul II, he concluded:

And so, today... on the basis of long personal experience of life, I say to you, dear young people: Do not be afraid of Christ! He takes nothing away, and he gives you everything. When we give ourselves to him, we receive a hundredfold in return. Yes, open, open wide the doors to Christ—and you will find true life.[18]

16   Pope Benedict XVI, Homily at the Beginning of His Pontificate (May 25, 2005).
17   Pope Benedict XVI, Homily at the Beginning of His Pontificate (May 25, 2005).
18   Pope Benedict XVI, Homily at the Beginning of His Pontificate (May 25, 2005).

Pope Francis also often reminds us: "He asks you to *leave behind what weighs down your heart*, to empty yourself of goods in order to make room for him."[19] Thus we will experience what all the saints did: God does not take anything away from us, but rather fills our heart with a peace and joy that the world cannot give.

By following this path, fear eventually yields to a deep gratitude: "I thank him who has given me strength for this, Christ Jesus our Lord, because he judged me faithful… though I formerly blasphemed and persecuted and insulted him; but I received mercy" (1 Tm 1:12–13). The fact that we all have a vocation shows how God's mercy is not hindered by our weaknesses and sins. He presents himself to us as *Miserando atque eligendo* (mercifully choosing), the episcopal motto of Pope Francis. Because, for God, choosing us and being merciful with us—overlooking our littleness—is one and the same thing.

As were Abraham, St. Paul, and all of Jesus' friends, we know that we are not only called and accompanied by God, but also sure of his help, convinced that "he who began a good work in you will bring it to completion at the day of Jesus Christ" (Phil 1:6). We know that our difficulties, although serious at times, do not have the last word. As St. Josemaría said: *when God our Lord plans some work for the benefit of mankind, he first thinks of the people he will use as instruments… and gives them the necessary graces.*[20]

---

19   Pope Francis, Homily at a Canonization (October 14, 2018). See also *Gaudete et Exsultate*, 32.

20   St. Josemaría, *Instruction*, March 19, 1934, 48.

God's call therefore is an invitation to trust. Only trust allows us to live without being enslaved by dependence on our own strength, our own talents, since we open ourselves to the marvel of living with the strength and talents of the one who called us. In the same way, when scaling a high mountain peak, we need to trust the one above us, with whom we might even share the same rope. The one who goes ahead of us shows us where to step and helps us when, if we were alone, we might let ourselves be overcome by panic or vertigo. That is how we walk along our path in life, with the difference that our trust isn't placed in someone like us, nor even in the best of friends; our trust is now placed in God himself, who always "remains faithful—for he cannot deny himself" (2 Tim 2:13).

You Will Blaze a Trail

"Abram went, as the LORD had told him" (Gen 12:4). Thus began the stage in his life that would change his existence forever. From that moment on, his life was guided by successive calls from God: to go from this place to that place, to flee from wicked men, to believe in the possibility of having a son, to see that son become part of his life, and then even to be willing to sacrifice him. Abraham's free response was always essential in order to keep saying yes to God. Likewise, the life of those who follow God is not only marked by closeness and communion with God, but also by a real, full, and continuous freedom.

Responding affirmatively to God's call not only gives our freedom a new horizon and its fullest meaning—"something great," which is love, as St. Josemaría said—it also requires that we exercise our freedom continually. Giving ourselves to God is not like getting on a "conveyor belt" that is directed by others and that carries us along—without our wanting it—until the end of our days; nor like getting on a railway with the track perfectly set out in advance, with no room for any surprises for the traveler.

Rather, throughout our lives we will find that fidelity to the first call requires new, sometimes costly, decisions from us. And we will realize that God's call spurs us to grow in our freedom each day. In order to fly high—as with any path of love—one needs wings clean of dirt and a great capacity to take responsibility for one's own life, which is so often enslaved by little things. In short, the greatness of God's invitation calls for a freedom that is just as great, enlarged by our response to grace and our growth in virtues, which make us more truly ourselves.

In the early years of his apostolic work, St. Josemaría used to tell the young people who came to him that everything still needed to be done, including the trail they needed to blaze. They were called to open up in the world the path that our Lord was indicating to them: *"[T]here are no roads made for you. You yourselves will make the way through the mountains, beating it out by your own footsteps."*[21] He was pointing to the "open" nature of every vocation, which needs to be discovered and cultivated.

---

21   St. Josemaría, *The Way* (New York: Scepter, 1982), no. 928.

Now, as then, responding to God's call means in a certain sense blazing a trail with our own footsteps. God never gives us a perfectly scripted plan. He didn't do so with Abraham or Moses, nor with the apostles. At the Ascension, he only told them: "Go into all the world and preach the gospel to the whole creation" (Mk 16:15). How were they to do so? And where? All this would only become clear little by little. In our case, too, the road will come into clearer focus as our life advances, as it is built through the wonderful alliance between God's grace and our own freedom. Throughout our lives, the vocation is "the history of an inexpressible dialogue between God and human beings, between the love of God who calls and the freedom of individuals who respond lovingly to him."[22] Our history will be an interweaving of our attentiveness to divine inspirations and our creativity to carry them out in the best way we can.

Our Lady is an example for all of us by her "yes" to God in Nazareth. And also because of her permanent attentiveness and obedience to God's will throughout her whole life, which was also marked by the "light-filled obscurity" of faith. "Mary kept all these things, pondering them in her heart" (Lk 2:19). Alongside her Son, our mother discovered what God wanted from her at every step of the way. That is why we also call Mary the perfect disciple. We entrust ourselves to her, so that she may be the star that always guides our steps.

---

22   St. John Paul II, Apostolic Exhortation on the Formation of Priests *Pastores Dabo Vobis* (March 25, 1992), 36.

CHAPTER 3
OUR TRUE NAME

Lucas Buch

The first book in the Bible begins with an account of God the creator, who brings creatures into existence with merely his word:

And God said, "Let there be light".… "Let there be a firmament in the midst of the waters".… "Let the earth put forth vegetation, plants yielding seed, and fruit trees".… "Let the earth bring forth living creatures according to their kinds: cattle and creeping things and beasts of the earth according to their kinds." (Gen 1:3, 6, 11, 24)

But when the moment comes to create the human being, something different happens. Rather than simply creating a species or kind of being, God creates a being made in his own image, a being called *personally* into existence, who is given a personal name and who God addresses personally.

If we turn from this account of creation to the last book in the Bible, we discover something surprising. Besides the name we receive from God when he creates us, we need to be given a new name at the end of our life. "To him who conquers I will give some of the hidden manna, and I will give him a white stone, with a new name written on the stone which no one knows except him who receives it" (Rev 2:17). How are we to understand this new name that will be given to us at the end of our life? We are faced here with the mystery of vocation—a personal mystery that unfolds as we advance on our path towards true life.

Both Free and Unfinished

A rose, an oak tree, or a horse doesn't need to make any decision to become what it is: it simply exists. It grows and reaches its fullness and finally disappears. But it's not the same with the human person.

As we grow, and especially during adolescence, we come to realize that we can't simply be "one more." Something urges us to become *someone* unique, with a name and surname, a distinct and unrepeatable person. We sense that we are in the world to achieve something, and that through our life we can make this world a better place. We aren't satisfied with knowing what we are or how things are, but rather feel urged to dream of *who* we would like to be and how we would like our world to be.

Some people will see this as being naïve, as a lack of realism that sooner or later needs to be overcome. Nevertheless, this urge to dream truly pertains to our highest self. For a Christian, the desire to be someone, with a name and surname, reveals how God has wanted to create us: as a being who is unrepeatable. He created the world and left it in the hands of our first parents, "to till it and keep it" (Gen 2:15). He wished to count on our work to preserve this world and make it shine forth in all its beauty, so that we will love it "passionately," as St. Josemaría liked to say.[1]

God does the same when he grants us the gift of life. He invites us to develop our own personality, and leaves this effort in our own hands. Therefore he wants us to put into play our personal freedom, our initiative, and all our abilities. "God wants something from you. God hopes in you," Pope Francis said in a World Youth Day address. "He is encouraging you to dream. He wants to make you see that, with you, the world can be different. For the fact is, unless you offer the best of yourselves, the world will never be different. This is the challenge"[2]

He Calls Us by Name

Simon accompanied his brother Andrew to listen to the Baptist. The journey from Galilee to Judea was a long one, but it was worth the effort. Something great seemed to be occurring there. Centuries had gone by since God had sent a prophet to his people, and now in John a new prophet seemed to have truly appeared among

---

1   See St. Josemaría, *Furrow* (New York: Scepter, 2002), 290; *Friends of God,* 206; and
     "Passionately Loving the World," in *Conversations with Saint Josemaría Escrivá* (New
     York: Scepter, 2007)*, 113–123.*

2   Pope Francis, Address at World Youth Day Prayer Vigil, Krakow (July 30, 2016).

them. Andrew encounters Jesus along the banks of the Jordan and spends an entire afternoon speaking with him. When he returns to his brother Simon, he tells him: "We have found the Messiah," and he brings Simon to Jesus (Jn 1:41–42). What must Simon have been thinking on the way there? Is it possible that the Messiah, the one sent by God, has finally arrived? Could the world they were living in be about to change, as Scripture prophesied? When they approached the Teacher, "Jesus looked at him, and said, 'So you are Simon the son of John? You shall be called Cephas' (which means Peter [rock])." Before the world could change, Simon's life had to change.

The Gospels show us Simon Peter's life as a continual discovery of Jesus' true identity, of the mission being entrusted to him. Soon after returning to Galilee, following those days spent with the Baptist, Jesus once again comes to Simon Peter, and asks him to put his boat out a little from the land so he can preach from it. Simon must have been a bit reluctant to do so, since he had just spent the whole night fishing and hadn't caught anything. When he finishes speaking with the people, Jesus makes a new request: "Put out into the deep and let down your nets for a catch" (Lk 5:4). It must have seemed absurd to Simon, since they had spent many hours that night fishing without success, and everyone knows that in the bright light of day fish refuse to enter the nets. But Simon obeys, and he sees his nets fill up with fish. Who must this man in his boat really be? "But when Simon Peter saw it, he fell down at Jesus' knees, saying, 'Depart from me, for I am a sinful man,

O Lord'" (Lk 5:8). And our Lord responds: "Do not be afraid; henceforth you will be catching men" (Lk 5:10).

Who is Simon? A fisherman from Galilee, like the men in his family had always been? He had spent years at this work and had become very good at it. He thought that this was his identity. But Jesus sheds unsuspected light on his life. Our Lord's closeness reveals his true self: a sinner, but a sinner God has singled out, on whom he wants to rely. Hearing this divine call, Peter and his brother, "when they had brought their boats to land, they left everything and followed him" (Lk 5:11). Benedict XVI reflected on this Gospel scene:

> Peter could not yet imagine that one day he would arrive in Rome and that here he would be a "fisher of men" for the Lord. He accepted this surprising call, he let himself be involved in this great adventure: he was generous; he recognized his limits but believed in the one who was calling him and followed the dream of his heart. He said "yes," a courageous and generous "yes," and became a disciple of Jesus.[3]

Later on, our Lord is more specific about the mission that will reshape his life: "And I tell you, you are Peter, and on this rock I will build my church, and the powers of death shall not prevail against it" (Mt 16:18). God's plan for us, his call to share our life with him, has the same transforming force as creation. Just as the human being's creation involves a personal call, so also each per-

3   Pope Benedict XVI, General Audience (May 17, 2006).

sonal call from God has a creative power able to transform reality. This is something so radical that it means for us receiving a *new name*, a new life. Who remembers today a fisherman who lived two thousand years ago by the shores of a Middle Eastern lake? And yet how many people venerate Peter, an apostle called by Christ and "the visible foundation of his Church"?[4]

The Hidden Treasure

The mission Jesus offers us can change our life and fill it with light. Therefore, the realization that God could be calling us is very attractive. But it is also deeply unsettling. For it can seem to us that if we are being called, if God is counting on us, we could lose our freedom. Now we can't choose any other path in life! The only possible path is the one he wants for us.

Reflecting on the history of Peter's life can help us here. When he decided to leave everything in order to follow Jesus, did he lose his freedom? Wasn't this the freest and most "freeing" decision in his life? Sometimes we can view freedom as above all the ability to choose, without being limited by anything. Nevertheless, viewed in this light, freedom is reduced to specific choices that affect us only briefly: whether to eat a hamburger or chicken, whether we should play football or basketball, whether we listen to this song or that one.

---

4   *Catechism of the Catholic Church*, 2nd ed. (Washington, DC: Libreria Editrice Vaticana–United States Conference of Catholic Bishops, 2000), 936.

But there are other types of choices that give a completely new direction to our life, making it freer and more joyful. This happens when we put our entire life on the line and decide who we want to be. Freedom is then seen in its true light, in its "freeing" capacity. These are no longer momentary decisions, but decisions that affect our whole life. For example, the decision to get married to a person who is seen as the greatest treasure the world can offer. Or similarly, the decision to become a doctor, knowing that this choice will require great effort and sacrifice. Giving ourselves to another person or taking on a mission entails renouncing everything else. Certainly, this will place conditions on our future choices. Nevertheless, this step isn't seen as a renunciation, but rather as risking one's life for a love or goal that will fill it with meaning. And thus, over time, our name is no longer only the one received at baptism: now it is also "the husband or the wife of…" or "Doctor…". Our name, our identity, takes on a clearer shape; our life takes on a clearer meaning and direction.

Jesus offers us a choice of exactly this type. He has created us with certain gifts and qualities that shape our way of being. Later, in the course of our life, he presents to us a "treasure," a mission that is "hidden" in our soul. "The kingdom of heaven is like treasure hidden in a field, which a man found and covered up; then in his joy he goes and sells all that he has and buys that field" (Mt 13:44). In reality, the treasure is himself—his unconditional love; and the mission is the same that he received from his Father. If I have discovered it, I don't need to seek any further. I can embrace it with my entire life, and let him shape every facet of it: like Peter, apostle, rock on which the Church is founded; like Paul, apostle to the Gentiles; like Mary, the handmaid of the Lord, mother of the Savior.

Embracing this mission—welcoming Jesus into our life and following him—leads us to set aside everything else. For nothing can free us as much as the truth about ourselves: *veritas liberabit vos*, "the truth will make you free" (Jn 8:32). Thus, we can say with St. Paul:

> But whatever gain I had, I counted as loss for the sake of Christ. Indeed I count everything as loss because of the surpassing worth of knowing Christ Jesus my Lord. For his sake I have suffered the loss of all things, and count them as refuse, in order that I may gain Christ and be found in him. (Phil 3:7–9)

Perhaps discovering how close Jesus is to us can be a bit unsettling at first—realizing that he wants to count on us. But when we stop to consider it, we see how what he is asking from us fits perfectly with who we are, with our aptitudes and experience. It seems as though we were born *for this*. The "new" name then is seen as something that was already there from the creation of the world. God has made us for this. Nevertheless, perhaps it can seem too much for us. "This treasure, this mission… for me? God truly has set his eyes *on me*?"

Putting into Play All My Gifts and Aptitudes

God doesn't call us only at a specific moment in our life: he does so constantly. In the same way, our response lasts our entire life, responding to his calls to love more fully each day, with an ever-renewed love. *Ever since you said Yes, time has broadened your horizons, giving them new and brighter colors and making them more beautiful every day. But you have to continue saying Yes.*[5]

St. Peter said yes to our Lord many times. When many of those who had followed the Teacher went away scandalized on hearing him speak about the Bread of Life (Jn 6:60–71); or when Jesus insisted on washing his feet, and it seemed absurd for him to do so (Jn 13:6–10); Peter remained alongside Jesus, professing once again his faith. Nevertheless, there was much that he failed to understand about our Lord. He continued to dream about a glorious manifestation of our Lord to the world, when he would show himself in his triumphant power and become famous throughout the whole world. It took him years to realize that this wasn't God's way of acting. He experienced the sadness of denying Jesus three times, being a traitor to him. He had to confront his own weakness. But in the end, he understood, because he never turned his eyes from Jesus. *Our Lord converted Peter, who had denied him three times, without even a reproach, with a look full of Love.*[6] For the vocation is, in the end, an invitation to look at Jesus, to let oneself be looked

---

5   St. Josemaría, *Furrow*, 32.
6   St. Josemaría, *Furrow*, 964

at by him, to share his life and strive to imitate him. And this leads to a self-giving, filled with love, of one's entire life.

Peter's call took on its definitive form that day by the shore of the Sea of Galilee, when he encountered the risen Jesus. He had the opportunity to ask for forgiveness and realized how much he loved him, with his poor heart, and told him so again. The Divine Master responded, "Feed my sheep" (Jn 21:17); and then he told Peter, "Follow me" (Jn 21:19). This summed up everything, because Peter had already discovered that following our Lord meant loving to the end, on a marvelous path of self-giving and service to everyone: a path, not a goal. The same path we have to travel each day in our life, alongside Jesus.

A Fulfilled Life

Peter died a martyr in Rome. Tradition places the site of his martyrdom, by crucifixion, on the Vatican Hill. When he learned of the sentence, he would surely have looked back on his whole life: His days as a young man, with his strong and determined temperament; his work as a fisherman in Galilee. And then his encounter with Jesus, and from then on, so many marvelous events! So much joy and suffering. So many people who had entered his life. So much love. Yes, his life had certainly changed greatly. And it had all been worth it.

On meeting Simon by the banks of the Jordan, our Lord saw not only a grown man, with certain characteristics. He saw in him Peter: the *rock* on which he would build his Church. And when he looks at us, he sees all the good that we are going to do in our own life. He sees our talents, our world, our history, and he offers us the possibility to help him, despite our littleness. He doesn't ask us to do impossible things, but simply that we follow him.

Our qualities are what they are, neither more nor less, and this way of being makes us well-suited to follow our Lord and serve him in the Church. With his help, we are called to find the best way to do so, each of us with the gifts God has given us:

> Having gifts that differ according to the grace given to us, let us use them: if prophecy, in proportion to our faith; if service, in our serving; he who teaches, in his teaching; he who exhorts, in his exhortation; he who contributes, in liberality; he who gives aid, with zeal; he who does acts of mercy, with cheerfulness. (Rom 12:6–8)

Peter left behind that fisherman from Bethsaida who was so sure of himself. And God made of him a mediator, with Christ, between heaven and earth. His life story has been repeated many times throughout the centuries. And this continues being true today. As Popr Francis told young people taking part in a prayer vigil with him: "May the Lord bless your dreams."[7]

Jesus' call draws out the best from each young man and woman, in order to place their life at the service of others and lead it to fulfilment. We see this in Peter. We too have discovered how much he loves us and is counting on us, and we want to be attentive to his

---

7   Pope Francis, Address at World Youth Day Prayer Vigil, Krakow (July 30, 2016).

call: today, and each day in our life. And thus, when we come face to face with him, he will give us "a white stone, with a new name written on the stone which no one knows except him who receives it" (Rev 2:17). And we will recognize our true name.

PART II
THE RESPONSE

CHAPTER 4

HOW DO WE DISCOVER OUR VOCATION?

José Brage

T he sun has set in Judea. Nicodemus comes to Jesus seeking answers for the restlessness in his heart. With his features lit by the flickering lamp flame, his dialogue with Jesus opens up a new and mysterious world to him. The Nazarene's replies to his questions leave him perplexed. Jesus assures him: "The wind blows where it wills, and you hear the sound of it, but you do not know whence it comes or whither it goes; so it is with every one who is born of the Spirit" (Jn 3:8). A vocation, every vocation, is a mystery, and discovering it is a gift of the Spirit.

The Book of Proverbs says: "Three things are too wonderful for me; four I do not understand: the way of an eagle in the sky, the way of a serpent on a rock, the way of a ship on the high seas, and the way of a man with a maiden" (Prv 30:18–19). Even more so,

who, without God's help, can decipher the workings of grace in a
soul, and discover the meaning and destiny of a life? Who, without
being guided by the gifts of the Holy Spirit, can know "whence
it comes or whither it goes"—the divine breath in the soul that is
often audible only as longing and restlessness, inklings and hopes?
This is something that totally surpasses us. Hence the first thing
we need in order to discern our personal calling is humility: falling
on our knees before the ineffable, opening our heart to the action
of the Holy Spirit, who is always able to surprise us.

    Therefore to discover our own vocation, or help someone else to
do so, it is impossible *to offer prefabricated formulas, or rigid methods
or rules.*[1] That would be like trying *to place rails on the ever original
action of the Holy Spirit,*[2] which "blows where it wills." Cardinal
Ratzinger was once asked, "How many paths are there for reaching
God?" With disarming simplicity he replied, "As many as there
are people."[3] There are as many histories of vocation as there are
men and women. Below we will try to point out some of the most
frequent signs for reaching a conviction about one's own vocation,
in order to help us to recognize them.

A Restless Heart

Nicodemus senses a restlessness in his heart. He has heard Jesus
preach and been moved by his words. Nevertheless, some of his

1   St. Josemaría, *Letter*, May 6, 1945, 42.

2   St. Josemaría, *Letter*, May 6, 1945, 42.

3   Joseph Ratzinger, *The Salt of the Earth* (San Francisco: Ignatius Press, 1997), p. 34.

teachings have scandalized him. Certainly, witnessing Jesus' miracles has amazed him, but he has also been unsettled by the authority with which Jesus expels the merchants from the temple, calling it "my Father's house" (Jn 2:16). Who would dare to speak like this? In his heart he senses a growing hope that he finds it hard to repress. Could this be the Messiah? But he is still assailed by questions and doubts. He can't bring himself to follow Jesus openly, although he wants to find answers to his questions. So, he goes to him at night: "Rabbi, we know that you are a teacher come from God; for no one can do these signs that you do, unless God is with him" (Jn 3:2). His heart is restless.

The same thing happens to other people in the Gospel, like that young man who came up to Jesus one day and asked: "Teacher, what good deed must I do, to have eternal life?" (Mt 19:16). He isn't satisfied with his life. His heart is uneasy. He senses that he is capable of doing more. Jesus tells him that he is right to be searching: "You lack one thing..." (Mk 10:21). We can also recall here the apostles Andrew and John. When Jesus sees them following him, he asks, "What do you seek?" (Jn 1:38). All of these people are "searchers." They are searching for a marvelous turn of events that will transform their life and make it an adventure. Their heart is open and hungry for more, filled with dreams and longings. Restless.

A young person once asked St. Josemaría how one sensed a vocation to his apostolate, Opus Dei. He replied: *It's not a matter of feeling, my son, although we realize when God is calling us. The heart is uneasy, unsatisfied…. You aren't happy with yourself!*[4] Often when searching for our own vocation, everything begins with this restlessness in the heart.

A Loving Presence

But what exactly is this restlessness? Where does it come from? In recounting the scene of the young man who draws close to our Lord, St. Mark says that Jesus, "looking upon him loved him" (Mk 10:21). He does the same with us. Somehow, we sense in our soul the "presence" of a special love choosing us for a unique mission. God makes himself present in our heart and seeks an "encounter," communion. But this has not yet been achieved, and hence our restlessness.

This loving presence of God in the soul can be manifested in various ways: a hunger for greater intimacy with him; the eagerness to satisfy, through our own life, God's thirst for souls; the desire to build up the Church, God's family in the world; the longing to see our talents truly bear fruit; the dream of alleviating so much suffering in every corner of the world; the awareness of how many gifts we have received: "Why have I received so much and others so little?"

God's call can also be revealed through apparently fortuitous events, which stir our heart and leave an imprint there. When reflecting on his own life, St. Josemaría said:

---

4   St. Josemaría, Notes from a Family Gathering, *Cronica*, 1974, vol. 1, p. 529.

Our Lord was preparing me in spite of myself, using apparently innocuous things to instill a divine restlessness in my soul. Thus I came to understand very well that love, so human and so divine, that moved St. Thérèse of the Child Jesus when, leafing through the pages of a book, she suddenly came upon a picture of one of the Redeemer's wounded hands. Things like that happened to me too—things that moved me and led me to daily Communion, to purification, to confession, and to penance.[5]

This loving presence is sometimes also discovered through people or ways of living the gospel that leave a lasting, divine imprint on our soul. Although at times it may be an unexpected event or encounter that changes our life, usually our calling takes shape through the way we have lived our life up to this moment. Finally, words from Sacred Scripture may engrave themselves on our heart and leave a loving savor that lasts our whole life. This is what happened to St, Teresa of Calcutta, for example, by hearing Jesus' cry on the Cross: "I thirst" (Jn 19:28); and to St. Francis Xavier, whose life was changed by Jesus' question: "For what will it profit a man, if he gains the whole world and forfeits his life?" (Mt 16:26).

But perhaps what is most characteristic of this restlessness in the heart is that it is marked by what we could call a "painful appeal." As St. Paul VI said, God's call comes to us as "a voice that is both unsettling and calming at the same time, a gentle and imperious

5   St. Josemaría, Meditation, February 14, 1964. Cited in Andrés Vázquez de Prada, *The Founder of Opus Dei*, vol. 1, p. 67.

voice, a bothersome and yet loving voice."[6] The call both attracts and repels us; it spurs us to abandon ourselves to divine love, while frightening us with the risk of our freedom. *We resist saying "yes" to God; we both want to and don't want to.*[7]

Connecting the Dots in Prayer

Nicodemus comes to Jesus, spurred by his restlessness. The lovable figure of our Lord has already entered his heart; he has already begun to love him, but he needs to speak with him. In the dialogue that follows, the Master opens up new horizons to him: "Truly, truly, I say to you, unless one is born of water and the Spirit, he cannot enter the kingdom of God" (Jn 3:5). He invites him to a new life, a new beginning: to be "born of water and the Spirit" (Jn 3:5). Nicodemus fails to understand our Lord's words, and he asks with simplicity, "How can this be?" (Jn 3:9). In this face-to-face encounter, he begins to realize who he is for Jesus, and who Jesus should be for him.

In order for the restlessness in our heart to take on its true meaning in the discerning of our vocation, it needs to be "read" and interpreted in prayer, in our dialogue with God. "Why is this happening to me now, Lord? What are you trying to tell me? Why does my heart have these longings and yearnings? Why am I so unsettled by this while those around me aren't affected? Why do

6   St. Paul VI, Homily (October 14, 1968).
7   St. Josemaría, Notes from a Family Gathering, *Cronica*, 1972, p. 460.

you love me so much? How can I make the best use of these gifts you have given me?" Only the habitual disposition of prayer will enable us to rightly grasp God's loving care—his providence—in the events in our life, in the people we have come to know, and even in how our character has been shaped, with our interests and abilities. It is as though God, throughout our life's path, had been "connecting the dots," which only now, in uniting them in prayer, take on the shape of a recognizable picture.

Benedict XVI said in this regard:

> The secret of the vocation lies in the relationship with God, in prayer that develops, precisely, in inner silence, in the capacity for listening, hearing that God is close. And this is true both before the decision, that is, at the time of deciding and setting out, and afterwards, if one wants to be faithful and to persevere on the way.[8]

Therefore, as we try to decide on our vocation, the first and most important thing is to draw close to Jesus in prayer and learn to see our own life with his eyes. Perhaps we will experience what happened to the blind man whose eyes Jesus anointed with saliva. At first, he sees with a clouded vision, and men look like trees that are walking. But he lets our Lord continue and ends up seeing everything clearly (see Mk 8:22–25).

---

8   Pope Benedict XVI, Meeting with Young People, Cathedral of Sulmona (July 4, 2010).

The "Detonator"

Two years after that nighttime encounter with Jesus, an event takes place that will force Nicodemus to make a decision and show himself openly as a disciple of our Lord. Urged on by the chief priests and Pharisees, Pilate crucifies Jesus of Nazareth. Joseph of Arimathea obtains permission to recover his body and bury it. St. John recounts: "Nicodemus also, who had at first come to him by night, came" (Jn 19:39). The Cross of our Lord, the abandonment by his disciples, and perhaps the example of Joseph of Arimathea's fidelity, challenge Nicodemus personally and force him to make a decision: Others are doing this; what am I going to do for Jesus?

A detonator is a small, sensitive, explosive device, usually set off by a fuse or electric spark, that detonates the more powerful and less sensitive main explosive. In the process of seeking one's vocation, there is often an event that acts as a "detonator" for all the restlessness our heart harbors, giving it a clear meaning and pointing out a path with the impetus to follow it. This event can be of many different types, and its emotional charge can be greater or smaller. But the important thing is that, like the restlessness in the heart, it needs to be "read" and interpreted in prayer.

The detonator can be a divine motion in the soul, or an unexpected encounter with a supernatural reality, as happened with Pope Francis when he was almost seventeen. It was during the month of September, and he was about to meet up with some friends to go out and have a good time. But he decided to stop for a moment in his parish church. There he saw a priest he didn't know, but whose recollected attitude of prayer impressed him, so he decided to go to confession with him.

> In that confession, something strange happened to me. I don't know what it was, but it changed my life; I would say that I was caught off guard. It was a surprise, the wonder of an encounter; I realized that I was being awaited. From that moment on for me, God is the one who "acts first." We seek him, but he seeks us first. We want to find him, but he finds us first.[9]

At times the detonator will be the example of a close friend: My friend has given himself to God, and what am I going to do? Or it can be a warm invitation to accompany our friend on a specific path: "Come and see," as Philip encouraged Nathanael (Jn 1:46). Or it can even be an apparently trivial event, but one charged with meaning for someone whose heart is restless. God makes use of even very small things to stir up our soul—as happened to St. Josemaría when, after a heavy snowfall, the love of God came in search of him.

Often, however, rather than a sudden "detonation," this process involves the slow maturing of faith and love, through prayer. Little by little, almost without realizing it, with God's light a person attains moral certitude about his or her vocation and reaches a decision, under the impulse of grace. St. John Henry Newman,

---

9   S. Rubin and F. Ambrogetti, *The Jesuit: Conversations with Cardinal Jorge Bergoglio*, SJ (Buenos Aires: Vergara, 2010), p. 45.

when recalling the process of his own conversion, wrote regarding his growing doubts about the truth of the Anglican faith:

> Certitude of course is a point, but doubt is a progress; I was not near certitude yet. Certitude is a reflex action; it is to know that one knows. I believe I had not that, till close upon my reception into the Catholic Church.... Who can determine when it is, that the scales in the balance of opinion begin to turn, and what was a greater probability in behalf of a belief becomes a positive doubt against it?[10]

The gradual process of maturing in the decision to give oneself that takes place, little by little and without a sudden shock, is in reality usually much surer than that provoked by the brilliant flash of an external sign, which can easily dazzle and confuse us.

In any case, when presented with this "inflection point" in our life, not only do we begin to see our path clearly; our will is also moved to undertake this path. As St. Josemaría wrote: *If you were to ask me how the divine call is perceived, how one becomes aware of it, I would say that it is a new outlook on life. It is as though a new light is lit within us, a mysterious impulse.*[11] The calling is light and impulse: light in our minds, illumined by faith, to "read" our life; impulse in our heart, enkindled with God's love, to want to follow our Lord's invitation, even though it may be with the "painful

---

10   St. John Henry Newman, *Apologia Pro Vita Sua* (New York: Macmillan, 1931), p. 233.

11   St. Josemaría, *Letter*, January 9, 1932.

appeal" that often marks God's concerns. Therefore, each person should ask not only for "light to see their path but also the strength to want to unite themselves to the divine will."[12]

The Help of Spiritual Direction

We don't know whether Nicodemus asked for advice from other disciples before or after going to see Jesus. Perhaps it was Joseph of Arimathea himself who encouraged him to follow Jesus openly, without fearing the other Pharisees. If so, he would have led him to his definitive encounter with Jesus. This is what spiritual accompaniment or direction involves: being able to rely on the advice of someone who walks with us; someone who tries to live in harmony with God, who knows us well and loves us.

It's true that the calling is always something between God and us. No one can see the vocation for us. No one can decide for us. God addresses us, invites us, and gives us the freedom to respond, as well as his grace to follow this path. Nevertheless, in this process of discerning and deciding, it is a great help to be able to rely on an expert guide—among other reasons, in order to confirm that we possess the required objective qualities needed to undertake this path, and to ensure an upright intention in our decision to give ourselves to God. Moreover, as the *Catechism* teaches, a good spiritual director can become a teacher of prayer: someone who helps

12   Msgr. Fernando Ocáriz, "Light to See, Strength to Want To," September 24, 2018. Available at opusdei.org.

us to read and interpret in our prayer the yearnings in our heart and the events in our life.[13] Thus we can be helped to clarify our own calling. In the end, it is someone who can perhaps tell us one day, as St. John told St. Peter, on recognizing the Person speaking to them from the shore: "It is the Lord!" (Jn 21:7).

In any case, this discernment is to a large extent a personal path, as is also the final decision. God himself leaves us free—even after the "detonator." Hence, once the first step has been taken, it is easy for doubts to reappear. God never stops accompanying us, but he remains at a certain distance. It is certain that he has done everything, and will continue doing it, but now he wants us to take the final step with full freedom, with the freedom of love. He doesn't want slaves, but children. And therefore he remains at a discreet distance, without forcing our conscience—almost, we might say, as an "observer." He watches us and waits patiently and humbly for our decision.

"[Y]ou will conceive in your womb and bear a son" (Lk 1:31). In the moment of silence that follows the announcement of the archangel St. Gabriel, the whole world seems to hold its breath. The divine message had been delivered. For years God's voice has been speaking softly in Our Lady's heart. But now God is silent, and he waits. Everything depends on the free response of that young girl in Nazareth. "And Mary said, 'Behold, I am the handmaid of the Lord; let it be to me according to your word'" (Lk 1:38). Years

---

13   *Catechism of the Catholic Church*, 2690.

later, at the foot of the Cross, Mary will receive from the hands of Nicodemus the dead body of her Son. How moved would this recent disciple have been to see, amid such immense sorrow, the mother of Jesus lovingly accept once again the path of God: "[L]et it be to me according to your word." How could one not give everything for a love that is so great?

CHAPTER 5

SO THAT THE
MUSIC PLAYS

THE VOCATION TO OPUS DEI

Eduardo Camino and Carlos Ayxelá

When Jesus spoke about the kingdom of God, he knew it was something quite different from what those listening to him might imagine—quite different also from what we might tend to imagine today. Hence, rather than giving a definition, he made use of parables: stories and images that invite us to enter more deeply into a mystery. For example, Jesus compares the kingdom of God to "a grain of mustard seed, which, when sown upon the ground, is the smallest of all the seeds on earth; yet when it is sown it grows up and becomes the greatest of all shrubs, and puts forth large branches, so that the birds of the air can make nests in its shade" (Mk 4:31–32). It is a small grain that disappears into the ground and is forgotten, but that never stops growing, while the world continues on its apparently separate course. It grows even at night, when no one is caring for it or paying attention.

In October 1928, God led St. Josemaría to discover a seed in his soul that only he could have placed there: a small grain meant to grow in the great field of the Church. A note written down a few months later sketches the "genetic code" of this seed: *Ordinary Christians. Dough being leavened. Ours is to be ordinary, natural. The means: everyday work. All saints! Silent self-giving.*[1] From the day God gave him the mission to care for this seed, St. Josemaría's only concern was to see it become a reality. And what was then simply a promise, a hope, today is a leafy tree that gives shelter to many souls and a rich savor to many lives.

The Desire to Be Holy Is What Is Normal

Pope Francis tells us: "Every saint is a message which the Holy Spirit takes from the riches of Jesus Christ and gives to his people."[2] St. Josemaría received a message that he embodied in his own life. He himself became the message, and his life and words began to challenge many people: *Don't let your life be sterile. Be useful. Blaze a trail. Shine forth with the light of your faith and of your love.... And*

---

1   St. Josemaría, *Intimate Notes*, 25. In *Opus Dei in the Church*, Pedro Rodriguez, Fernando Ocáriz, José Luis Illanes (Four Courts Press, 1994), p. 133.

2   Pope Francis, Apostolic Exhortation on the Call to Holiness *Gaudete et Exsultate* (March 19, 2018), 21.

light up all the ways of the earth with the fire of Christ that you carry in your heart.[3]

He carried this fire inside, as one of the first followers of St. Josemaría ordained to the priesthood, José Luis Múzquiz, quickly realized. The first time he spoke with St. Josemaría, he heard something that perhaps he had never heard before: the possibility to be an apostle in his work. And right away St. Josemaría added: *The only real love is God's Love; the others are little loves.* These words deeply impressed him: "One could see that it came from the depths of his soul, from a soul in love with God. The mental circuits I had in place all melted down."[4]

In a Mass of thanksgiving for the beatification of this soul in love with God, then-Cardinal Ratzinger said, with his characteristic simplicity and depth:

> The meaning of the word "holy" has undergone a dangerous narrowing over the course of time, and this certainly still influences it today. It makes us think of the saints whose statues and paintings we see at the altars, of miracles and heroic virtues, and it suggests that holiness is for a chosen few, among whom we cannot be included. Then we leave holiness to the few, of an unknown number, and content ourselves with being just the way we are.

3   St. Josemaría, *The Way*, 1.
4   St. Josemaría, *The Way: A Critical-historical Edition*, commentary on point 417.

Amidst this spiritual apathy, Josemaría Escrivá issued a wake-up call, shouting: No! Holiness is not something extraordinary but rather ordinary; it is what is normal for every baptized person. Holiness does not mean the sort of heroism that it is impossible to imitate; rather it has a thousand different forms and can become a reality anywhere, in any job. It is what is normal.[5]

The natural thing, then, for a Christian is the desire to be holy. St. Josemaría wrote, when still a young priest: *Saints are not abnormal cases to be studied by a modernistic doctor. They were—they are—normal with flesh like yours. And they conquered.*[6] The call to holiness entails an awareness of the "normality" of sanctity, with the desire to become an "interpreter" of this simple message, of this music. The "musical score" for this message already exists: the life and preaching of St. Josemaría; the proclamation of the universal call to holiness by Vatican II;[7] the magisterium of the recent popes, who have all stressed this teaching;[8] and above all the Gospels. But this music needs to be heard in every corner of the world, with the infinite variations that still need to become a reality: the individual lives of so many Christians.

---

5   Joseph Ratzinger, Homily (May 19, 1992).

6   St. Josemaría, *The Way*, 133.

7   St. Paul VI, Dogmatic Constitution on the Church *Lumen Gentium* (October 21, 1964), 40. Vatican website. www.vatican.va.

8   See St. John Paul II, Apostolic Exhortation on the Laity *Christifideles Laici* (December 30, 1988), 16–17; Pope Benedict XVI, General Audience (April 13, 2011); and, more recently, Pope Francis' *Gaudete et Exsultate*.

So Close That We Live with Him

In inspiring the apostolic work of St. Josemaría, our Lord presented his Church with a path, a spirituality "designed" to be embodied in every type of daily setting. *Far away on the horizon Heaven seems to meet the earth. Do not forget that where Heaven and earth really meet is in your heart of a child of God.*[9] Hence, although the vocation to live holiness in all aspects of life spurs a person to have initiative in seeking to better the world, it doesn't lead above all to doing things, or to doing more things than what one was already doing. Rather it leads above all to doing them in a different way, being *with God* in everything we do, striving to share everything with Him.

> *My children, our vocation is to follow Christ. And to follow Him so closely that we live with Him, like the first Twelve, so close to Him that we identify with Him, that we live his Life, until a moment comes, if we haven't hindered it, when we can say with St. Paul: "It is now no longer I who live, but Christ who lives in me.*[10]

One of the first married members of Opus Dei recalls his surprise when St. Josemaría told him: *God is calling you to the path of contemplation.* As a married person with children who had to work hard to support his family, this was "a true discovery."[11] St. Josemaría

---

9   St. Josemaría, *Furrow*, 309.
10   St. Josemaría, *In Dialogue with the Lord* (Scepter, 2018), p. 23.
11   Victor García Hoz, "Mi encuentro con Monseñor Escrivá de Balaguer," in R. Serrano, ed., *Así le vieron* (Madrid: Rialp, 1992), p. 83.

advised another person: *Talk with our Lord; tell Him: "I'm tired, Lord. I'm at the end of my strength. Lord, this isn't going well. How would you do it?"*[12] This is what contemplation in the middle of the world involves: looking at the real world with love, while also looking at God, in an unbroken dialogue. St. Josemaría summed up this beautiful challenge in a striking phrase: *the more within the world we are, the more we must be God's.*[13] And this closeness, this deep friendship with him, gives rise to two features that, although not exclusive to the vocation to the Work, have a special importance for those God calls to this path: the call to be apostles, to make Christ known; and the mission to transform and reconcile the world with God through one's work.

Before considering these features, however, a question naturally arises. If, as St. Josemaría always insisted, and as the Pope recently reminded us, sanctity is meant for everyone; if our Lord gives all Christians the mandate to make the gospel known, what is specific then to the vocation to Opus Dei as a response to the call to find God in the middle of the world?

This is fairly easy to explain if we keep in mind that the various vocations found in Christian life are specifications, modalities, or channels of the life and vocation communicated by baptism. Specifically, "the vocation to Opus Dei 'takes up, welcomes, channels' the self-giving or dedication to God and to others that is required by the

---

12   St. Josemaría, Notes from a Family Get-Together in Valladolid, October 22, 1972.

13   St. Josemaría, *The Forge* (New York: Scepter, 2002), 740.

Christian vocation; the only special element 'added' is precisely the 'channel'—that this dedication be carried out by forming part of a specific institution of the Church (Opus Dei), which has a specific spirituality and also specific means of formation and apostolate,"[14] aimed specifically at serving God and other men and women through work and ordinary, daily realities. Or to put it another way: those who discover and welcome the call to Opus Dei decide to give their life for others (which is the essence of Christian life), along a specific path, led by God's hand and with the help of a great family. And therefore, they are ready to do all they can on their part to enable this charism to nourish their interior life, illumine their intellect, and enrich their personality, so that they can truly find God in their life and share this wonderful discovery with others.

The divine illumination received on the second of ,October 1928, and others that followed, showed St. Josemaría that he needed to dedicate his life to fostering among ordinary Christians—men and women who live in the middle of the world, carrying out a wide variety of different jobs—the awareness that all are called to holiness and apostolate. And he was to do this through an institution, Opus Dei, made up of ordinary Christians who, in accepting the divine call to make this ideal their own, give witness with their own life to the marvelous possibility, with the help of grace, to put it into practice, even amid their own limitations.

---

14   Msgr. Fernando Ocáriz, "Vocation to Opus Dei as a Vocation in the Church," in *Opus Dei in the Church*, p. 103.

All Who Have a Big Heart

On the path from Bethany to Jerusalem, Jesus is hungry. He looks for something to eat and stops at a fig tree (Mt 21:18–19). *Jesus approaches the fig tree: he approaches you, he approaches me. Jesus hungers, he thirsts for souls. On the Cross he cried out* Sitio!, 'I thirst' *(Jn 19:29). He thirsts for us, for our love, for our souls and for all the souls we ought to be bringing to him, along the way of the Cross which is the way to immortality and heavenly glory.*[15]

The vocation to the Work entails a strong "contagion" of this hunger and thirst of God. When St. Josemaría was struggling to get the first residence of the Work underway, some people advised him not to be in such a hurry. While on retreat he wrote down: *Hurry. It's not hurry. It's that Jesus is urging us on.*[16] He was urged on, like St. Paul, by Christ's love (see 2 Cor 5:14). With this same serene urgency God wants us to call at the heart of each man and woman: "Wake up to the fact that you are loved!"[17] And to do so in a normal, natural way; loving and letting oneself be loved by everyone; helping and serving them; passing on what we know; learning from them; sharing challenges and projects, problems and worries; creating bonds of friendship. Right there where we work, rest, and shop, we can be leaven, salt, light for the world.

---

15   St. Josemaría, *Friends of God*, 202.
16   St. Josemaría, *Intimate Notes*, 1753, cited in Andrés Vázquez de Prada, *The Founder of Opus Dei*, vol. I, p. 394.
17   St. John Paul II, *Crossing the Threshold of Hope*, p. 19.

God doesn't call "superheroes" to his Work. He calls normal people, people who have a big, magnanimous heart, in which all men and women find a place. In a document from the first years, St. Josemaría wrote about those who could receive God's call to the Work: *There is no room in the Work for those who are selfish, cowardly, indiscreet, pessimistic, tepid, foolish, lazy, timid, frivolous. There is room for the sick, God's favorites, and for all those who have a big heart, even though their frailties may have been quite big.*[18] Those who discover that God is calling them to Opus Dei can be people with defects and limitations, but they need to have big ideals, the eagerness to love and to enkindle in others God's love.

Loving the World as God Loves It

"God so loved the world that he gave his only Son, that whoever believes in him should not perish but have eternal life" (Jn 3:16). God loves the world he has created "passionately." Hence it isn't an obstacle to holiness but rather its "native place." The core of Opus Dei's message is contained in this conviction: we can be holy not *despite* living in the world, but rather by taking advantage of it, being deeply immersed in it—because the world, this mysterious amalgam of greatness and wretchedness, love and hate, rancor and forgiveness, war and peace, "waits with eager longing for the revealing of the sons of God" (Rom 8:19).

---

18   St. Josemaría, *Instruction*, 1 April 1934, 65.

When speaking about mankind's relationship with the world, Genesis employs two verbs: "care for" and "cultivate" (see Gen 2:15, NABRE). With the first, which is also used to express the fulfillment of the commandments, we are shown our responsibility for the world, and the fact that we can't make use of it in a despotic way. While the second verb, "cultivate," which means both "to work" (usually the earth) as well as "to offer cult" (see Num 8:11), unites work to worship. By working we not only attain self-fulfillment; we also offer a pleasing worship to God, because we love the world as he loves it. Therefore, sanctifying our work means, in the end, making the world more beautiful, making room in it for God.

He himself has wanted to keep and cultivate the world that came forth good from his hands as Creator, by working with the hands of a man, of a creature. For centuries our Lord's years of hidden life in the workshop at Nazareth were viewed as years of obscurity, lacking in light. But in the light of the spirit of the Work they become *filled with bright sunlight that illumines our days and imbues them with meaning.*[19] Therefore, St. Josemaría encouraged his sons and daughters to reflect often on these hidden years of work, which recall for us the "hidden and silent" growth of the grain of wheat. This is how Jesus grew up—later he will even compare himself to the grain of wheat (Jn 12:24)—in the workshop of Joseph and his mother, in that workshop that was also a home.

---

19   St. Josemaría, *Christ is Passing By*, 14.

The Holy Family's humble life shows us that there are jobs that, although they may seem of little importance to earthly eyes, in God's eyes have immense value, because of the love and care put into them, with the desire to be useful. Hence "sanctifying work does not mean *doing something holy* while working, but rather *making the work itself holy*."[20] Thus "work humanly well done has become a healing 'salve' for people's eyes so that they can discover God in every circumstance and facet of life. Moreover, this has happened right in our times when materialism is bent on turning work into mud which blinds people and prevents them from looking at God."[21]

To bear fruit, the grain needs to hide in the ground, to disappear. This is how St. Josemaría saw his own life: *My role is to hide and disappear, so that only Jesus shines forth.*[22] This is also how God wants all the men and women heto see their lives: like the first Christians—normal, ordinary people who, if they raised their voices, it wasn't to seek the applause of others but rather to make God shine forth. People who, above all, *lived in union with Christ and who made him known to others… sowers of peace and joy, the peace and joy that Jesus has brought to us.*[23]

---

20   Msgr. Fernando Ocáriz, *Naturaleza, gracia y gloria* (Eunsa, 2000), p. 263.

21   Bl. Alvaro del Portillo, *Letter*, September 9, 1975.

22   St. Josemaría, *Letter*, January 28, 1975.

23   St. Josemaría, *Christ is Passing By*, 30.

CHAPTER 6

GIVING OUR LIVES FOR OUR FRIENDS

THE VOCATION TO CELIBACY

Carlos Villar

"So God created man in his own image, in the image of God he created him; male and female he created them" (Gen 1:27). This is the first creation account in Genesis of the origin of man and woman, with God creating them at the same time. Both possess the same dignity, because they are his living image. The second account focuses again on this event (Gen 2:7–25), but with a "slow-motion camera," as it were. God creates man first and places him in the garden of Eden. The beauty of the newly created world shines forth: the sky, the waters of the sea, the rivers that flow through the mountains, and the trees of all types. It is an extraordinary scene, but Adam feels lonely.

To remedy his solitude, the Lord creates a whole host of living creatures to populate Paradise: the birds of the air, the fish swimming in the seas, the land animals. But all this still seems insufficient to the man. It is then that God decides to grant him *a* "helper fit for him" (Gen 2:18), and from the man's own rib he creates the woman. Finally, Adam discovers eyes that return a look like his own: "This at last is bone of my bones and flesh of my flesh; she shall be called Woman, because she was taken out of Man" (Gen 2:23). This encounter fills him with joy, but above all it sheds light on his own identity: it tells him in a new way who he is. Something was missing for the man, which only another person could give him.

"It Is Not Good for Man to Be Alone"

These pages in Genesis provide fundamental truths about the human being that are expressed, rather than by theoretical reflections, by a narrative, with a symbolic language. The solitude of Adam therefore has a deep anthropological meaning. St. John Paul II said that every man and woman shares in that "original solitude," and at some moment in life they have to face it.[1] When God says "it is not good that the man should be alone" (Gen 2:18), this actually refers to both of them:[2] both the man as well as the woman need a

1   See St. John Paul II, General Audiences (October 10, 1979; October 24 1979; and October 31, 1979).

2   See St. John Paul II, General Audience (October 10, 1979), 2.

helper to escape from this solitude, a way to walk together toward the fullness that they lack. And this is marriage.

When, centuries later, Jesus reminds the Pharisees of how it was "from the beginning," he was referring precisely to this passage of the Bible (see Mt 19:1–12). Christian marriage is God's call inviting a man and a woman to walk together toward him. And not only together, but also *through one another*. The spouse is, for a married person, a totally necessary path towards God—a path where the flesh becomes the setting for a loving communion and self-giving, the matter and space for sanctification. Marital love is thus an encounter of bodies and souls that embellishes and transfigures human affection, giving it, with the grace of the sacrament, a supernatural value.

At the same time, the love between a man and a woman points to something beyond itself. When it is true, it is always a *path toward* God, not the goal. The goal continues being the fullness that is found only in him. Therefore, the fact that someone who is married might sense that "original solitude" at times isn't surprising. Nevertheless, this sensation doesn't mean, as it is sometimes interpreted, that love has come to an end and that a different story of love should begin, because neither would that story be sufficient. Rather it is a sign that the human heart has a thirst that can only be quenched completely in the infinite love of God.

Knowing That One Is Not Alone

In that same dialogue on marriage, after recalling the teaching in Genesis, Jesus goes a step further. The mutual self-giving of a man and a woman is a beautiful path leading to God. Nevertheless, it is not the only possible path. Our Lord speaks of those who, through a special gift, renounce marriage "for the sake of the kingdom of heaven" (Mt 19:12). He himself traveled this path: Jesus remained celibate. In his life he had no need for any mediation between God and himself: "I and the Father are one (Jn 10:30); "I am in the Father and the Father in me" (Jn 14:11). And Jesus not only traveled this path; he himself wanted to become the Way so that many other persons might love in the same way, "which can only find meaning in God."[3]

The history of the Church is filled with the stories of people who have welcomed Jesus' call to identify themselves with him in this way: something central to Jesus, deeply rooted in his life, even though it is not meant for all Christians. Those who from the first centuries answered the call to celibacy did not hold marriage in contempt. Perhaps that other path in life had even attracted them as much as the one they decided to take. But for that very reason, because they saw married life as something beautiful, they could offer their choice to God with a radiant joy. *Only among those who understand and value in all its depth human love*, St. Josemaría said, *can there arise that other ineffable understanding of which Jesus spoke*

---

3   Pope Benedict XVI, Address to the Roman Curia (December 22, 2006).

(cf. Mt 19:11). It is a pure gift of God which moves a person to dedicate body and soul to him, to offer him an undivided heart, without the mediation of earthly love.[4] In some way, those called by God to celibacy are led to discover the *source* and *goal* of all authentic love. They experience in a special way the love that filled the heart of Jesus and that has been poured out on his Church.

Hence celibacy is a path that reflects the gratuitous love of the One who always takes the first step (see 1 Jn 4:19). Although celibate persons seem to surrender their freedom when they offer to God the possibility of establishing a family, in reality they enlarge it. Their abandonment into God's hands, their willingness to leave "houses or brothers or sisters or father or mother or children or lands" (Mt 19:29) for his sake, makes them in a special way "free to love."[5] Like a married person, they need to keep custody over their heart, so that the love they bear within doesn't turn away from God, and so they can give it to others. But their self-giving isn't focused on the person of the spouse, but on Christ, who sends them out to the whole world to transmit *the beating of his most loving heart*[6] to the specific people around them.

This was Jesus' life. He didn't feel lonely, because he knew he was always accompanied by his Father: "Father, I thank thee that thou hast heard me. I knew that thou hearest me always" (Jn 11:41–42). For us, however, the risk of loneliness remains. But

---

4   St. Josemaría, *Conversations*, 122.
5   Msgr. Fernando Ocáriz, *Letter*, February 14, 2017, 8.
6   St. Josemaría, *The Way* (New York: Scepter, 1982), 884.

when Christ truly fills our heart, we no longer feel alone. Hence St. Josemaría said that God had given him *the psychological feeling of never being alone, either humanly or supernaturally.*[7] In words that reflect his own experience, he wrote, *The human heart is endowed with an enormous coefficient of expansion. When it loves, it opens out in a crescendo of affection that overcomes all barriers.*[8]

John, a Celibate Heart

At the Last Supper, a few hours before offering up his life, Jesus opens his heart to the apostles: "Greater love has no man than this, that a man lay down his life for his friends" (Jn 15:13). These words that express his love for all mankind are also a call. Our Lord tells the apostles, "I have called you friends" (Jn 15:15). They, like all men and women, are recipients of his love "to the end" (Jn 13:1). But they are also friends in a special way. "The Friend" invites them to do what he will do: to also give their life for their friends.[9] These words are undoubtedly at the origin of every Christian vocation, but they have always resounded in a special way in the hearts of those who have followed Christ by leaving behind everything.

The Cross will be the place of the greatest manifestation of love. In this sublime scene, together with Mary and the holy women, the figure of the apostle John is shown clearly to us. *At the moment of*

---

7   St. Josemaría, *In Dialogue with the Lord* (Scepter, 2018), p. 66.

8   St. Josemaría, *The Way of the Cross*, Station 8.

9   St. Josemaría at times referred to Jesus as "the Friend." See, for example, *The Way*, 422; and *Christ is Passing By*, 93.

truth, they all fled, except for John who truly loved with deeds. Only the adolescent, the youngest of the Apostles, can be found next to the Cross. The others didn't find within themselves that love as strong as death.[10] Right from the dawn of adolescence, his heart strongly sensed Jesus' love. We know how dear the memory was to him of the day he first met our Lord: *John's eyes meet Christ's. He follows Him and asks: Teacher, where do you live? And he went with Him, and spent the whole day with the Teacher. Years later he recounts it with an enchanting candor, like an adolescent keeping a diary who pours out his heart and records even the exact hour:* hora autem erat quasi decima.... *He recalls the precise moment when Christ looked at him, when Christ attracted him, when he couldn't resist Christ, when he fell in love with Christ.*[11]

It is easy to imagine how Jesus, on the Cross, would be moved to see the young disciple who "had lain close to his breast at the supper" (Jn 21:20). Perhaps he wasn't surprised to see his mother. In one way or another, she had always been at his side. But next to her our Lord finds a friend: John. Amid all that anguish, their eyes meet. What an immense joy it must have been for Jesus' heart! And it is then, the Gospel tells us, on seeing him next to his mother, that our Lord made John part of the unique relationship that existed between Mary and himself: "When Jesus saw his mother, and the disciple whom he loved standing near, he said to his mother,

10   St. Josemaría, *Christ is Passing By*, 2 (cf. *Song* 8:6).
11   St. Josemaría, Notes from a Get-Together with Young People, July 6, 1974.

'Woman, behold your son!' Then he said to the disciple, 'Behold your mother!'" (Jn 19:26–27).

Years later John would write: "We love, because he first loved us" (1 Jn 4:19). This surprising statement stemmed from his personal experience. John knew he was deeply loved by Jesus. This reality imbued his whole life and gave it new meaning: to bring that same love to the whole world. The apostle John, said St. John Henry Newman,

> had the unspeakable privilege of being the *friend of Christ*. Thus he was taught to love others; first his affection was concentrated, then it was expanded. Next he had the solemn and comforting charge of tending our Lord's Mother, the Blessed Virgin, after His departure. Do we not here discern the secret sources of his especial love of the brethren? Could he, who first was favored with his Savior's affection, then trusted with a son's office towards His Mother, could he be other than a memorial and pattern (as far as man can be), of love, deep, contemplative, fervent, unruffled, unbounded?"[12]

Awakening Hearts

Giving one's whole heart to God is not simply the result of a personal decision: it is a *gift*, the gift of celibacy. Similarly, its defining

---

12   St. John Henry Newman, "Love of Relations and Friends," *Parochial and Plain Sermons* 2, sermon 5.

mark is not renunciation, but rather the love that is discovered: [*His*] *Love… is well worth any love!*[13] The heart senses an unconditional Love, a Love that was awaiting it, and wants to dedicate itself to him in an unconditional, exclusive way. And not simply in order to experience it, but to *give it* as well to many other persons. Like St. John, who not only enjoyed the love of Jesus, but tried to ensure that this same love might spread throughout the whole world. For the beloved disciple, this was the natural consequence: "if God so loved us, we also ought to love one another" (1 Jn 4:11).

At times celibacy is viewed above all as the dedication of our time, as though this total dedication was justified by a question of effectiveness in advancing certain apostolic works, unhampered by other commitments. Nevertheless, that is a simplistic view. Celibacy is not the result of practical considerations about availability for evangelization, but rather a calling from Christ. It is an invitation to share in a special way in the life of his own heart: to love like Christ, to forgive like Christ, to work like Christ; even more, to be Christ himself—*ipse Christus*—for all souls. Therefore,

> the solely pragmatic reasons, the reference to greater availability, is not enough: such a greater availability of time could easily become also a form of egoism that saves a person from the sacrifices and efforts demanded by the reciprocal acceptance and forbearance in matrimony. Thus,

13   St. Josemaría, *The Way*, 171.

it could lead to a spiritual impoverishment or to hardening of the heart.[14]

Celibacy, then, is not solitude within an ivory tower, but rather a calling to accompany and awaken many hearts. How many people there are in the world who do not feel important, who think their lives have no value, and who at times fall into strange practices, because deep down they are seeking a bit of love! Those who receive the gift of celibacy know they are also in the world to draw close to all these people and reveal God's love to them, to remind them of their infinite value. Thus, the celibate heart is fruitful in the same way the fruitful and redeeming heart of Jesus is. It strives to discover in each person the same good that our Lord discovered in those who drew close to him. It doesn't see a sinner, a leper, a contemptible publican, but rather a beloved creature of God, chosen by him, of immense value.

Thus, even though those who live celibacy don't have natural children, they become capable of a deep and real fatherhood or motherhood. They are a father, or mother, of many children, because "paternity means giving life to others."[15] They know they are in the world to truly care for others, to show them, with their life and helpful words, that only God can quench their heart's thirst.

Our world in which God appears at best as a hypothesis but not as a concrete reality, needs to rest on God in the

14   Pope Benedict XVI, Address to the Roman Curia (December 22, 2006).
15   Pope Francis, Homily in Santa Marta (June 26, 2013).

most concrete and radical way possible. It needs a witness to God that lies in the decision to welcome God as a "land" where one finds one's own existence. For this reason, celibacy is so important today, in our contemporary world, even if its fulfilment in our age is constantly threatened and questioned.[16]

A Gift Called to Grow Day by Day

The divine gift of celibacy is not like a magic charm that brings about an immediate and permanent change. Rather, God grants it as a seed that needs to grow gradually in "good soil." Like every vocation, celibacy is a gift and a task. It is a path. Therefore, it is not enough to make the decision to dedicate oneself to be celibate for the kingdom of heaven for the heart to be automatically transformed. A continuous effort is needed to root out the weeds, to watch out for insects and parasites. Divine grace always acts upon nature without negating it or taking its place. In other words, God counts on our freedom and our personal history. And it is precisely there, in that mixture of human soil and divine grace, that the beautiful gift of a virginal heart silently grows. Where it grows… or where it is lost.

Like the younger son in the parable, even those called to a greater intimacy with God can one day feel jaded and empty. That young man decided to go off to a distant land (see Lk 15:13), because in his father's house he felt an inner emptiness. He needed to reach rock bottom, so that finally he would open his eyes and realize the state of slavery into which he had fallen. It is noteworthy that, according to the Gospel text, the reason for his return was not very spiritual. He was hungry, with a physical hunger. He missed the savory bread of his father's house. When he finally returned, his father was waiting for him and "ran and embraced him and kissed him" (Lk 15:20). The son had imagined facing almost a formal judgment (Lk 15:18–19); instead, he finds a loving embrace. He discovers—perhaps more clearly than ever—his deepest identity: he is the *son* of such a good Father.

At other times, feeling jaded can take on a more insidious form. While remaining in the father's house, one might feel more like a servant than a son—like the elder brother in the parable, who "was living at home, but he was not free, because his heart was elsewhere."[17] In both cases, the path to escape from sadness is to turn one's eyes to the Father and his love for us. God satisfies the hunger of the soul with the bread of the Eucharist, in which we find the One who has become one of us, so that we may love him as a Friend. There we can keep our heart enkindled with a love as "strong as death" (Song 8:6).

John stayed next to the cross of Jesus, and was also present at his ascension into heaven, "that day on which an apparent departure was in truth the beginning of a new nearness."[18] Jesus had to

---

17   Msgr. Fernando Ocáriz, *Letter*, January 9, 2018, 9.

18   Cardinal Joseph Ratzinger, "El comienzo de una nueva cercanía," in *El resplandor de Dios en nuestro tiempo* (Barcelona: Herder, 2008), p. 185.

separate himself physically from his disciples, whom he had loved to the end, in order to be able to love them even more closely, and to love each of the persons who would come to believe in him. This is the secret of a celibate heart: leaving behind a love on this earth in order to fill the whole world with the light of Christ's love.

CHAPTER 7

RESPONDING
TO LOVE

THE VOCATION TO MARRIAGE

Carlos Ayxelá

When St. Josemaría first began to speak about a vocation to marriage, almost a century ago now, uniting these two concepts would disconcert people, if not cause them to laugh; it was like speaking about a wingless bird or a square wheel. *You laugh because I tell you that you have a "vocation to marriage"? Well, you have just that—a vocation.*[1] In the mentality of that era, and even at times today, "to have a vocation" meant to leave behind what is normal in life in order to be able to serve God and the Church. And for the majority of people, what is normal is to have a family, children, a home, a job, purchases, bills, washing machines, leftovers in the fridge, and so on.

---

1   St. Josemaría, *The Way*, 27.

This list, as varied and unforeseeable as life itself, not only fits in the "square wheel" of the vocation to marriage, but finds there its best expression. The view of *marriage as a real call from God*[2] stems directly from the conviction that God blesses the normality of family life and wants to "dwell" there. "Thou dwellest in the holy place, the praise of Israel," says the Psalm that Jesus prayed on the Cross (Ps 21:4, Douay Rheims A). God, the Holy One, wants to live in the midst of the most normal lives of families—lives called to become, through the affection expressed there, a praise to him: to become a "heaven," despite all the unavoidable defects of this provisional site that is our earthly life.

May You Have a Good Journey

That young man laughed when he heard the words "a vocation to marriage," but he also became thoughtful. And he was given some specific advice: *Commend yourself to St. Raphael that he may keep you pure, as he did Tobias, until the end of the way.*[3] St. Josemaría makes reference here to the only story in the Bible about this archangel, for whom he had a special affection; so much so that very early on he entrusted to St. Raphael his apostolate with young people.[4] *The*

---

2   St. Josemaría, *Christ is Passing By*, 30. Cf. nos. 22–30, comprising the homily "Marriage: A Christian Vocation."

3   St. Josemaría, *The Way*, 27. See also no. 360.

4   See St. Josemaría, *Intimate Notes*, 1697 (October 10, 1932), in Andrés Vázquez de Prada, *The Founder of Opus Dei*, vol. 1.

book of Tobit is enchanting,[5] he once said. Although the entire book is the narration of a journey, it allows us to enter deeply into the lives of two homes, and to witness the birth of a third one. And even the journey itself shares in this atmosphere of a home, with a small detail that artists have not failed to notice down through the centuries. This book is the only place in Scripture where we see a household dog, who accompanies Tobias and St. Raphael along their entire journey (see Tob 6:1; 11:4).

When Tobias is about to leave, his father blesses him with these words: "God who dwells in heaven will prosper your way, and may his angel attend you" (Tob 5:16). St. Josemaría paraphrased these words when giving his blessing to those about to undertake a journey: *May the Lord be on your path, and may his Angel go with you.*[6] The true journey, the most decisive one, is the path of life, when husband and wife mutually give themselves to one another in marriage, responding to a dream of God that goes back to the origin of the world.[7] How important it is, then, to help young people discover, and to rediscover after journeying for many years,

5   St. Josemaría, Notes from a Meditation, October 12, 1947, in *While He Spoke to Us on the Way*, p. 31.

6   See St. Josemaría, Notes from a Meditation, October 12, 1947: "This is the formula I chose as the blessing for a journey, adding to it an invocation to our Lady: *Beata Maria intercedente, bene ambules: et Dominus sit in itinere tuo, et Angelus eius comitetur tecum* [Through our Lady's intercession, may you have a good journey, and may the Lord be on your path, and may his Angel go with you]."

7   St. John Paul II called marriage "the primordial sacrament" (see General Audiences, October 20 1982 and May 23 1984).

"the beauty of the vocation to form a Christian family":[8] the call to a holiness that is not second-class but first-class.

When Life Truly Begins

A person's vocation is born from a simple discovery that brings with it many consequences: the conviction that the meaning, the truth of our life is not found in living for ourselves, for our own concerns, but for others. We discover that we have received so much love in our life and that we are called to do the same: to give love. Only thus will we truly find ourselves. We must not only give love in our free moments, to tranquilize our conscience, but make love the central goal of our life, the center of gravity for all our other concerns.

Before and after his marriage with Sarah, the young man Tobias receives some advice in this regard, with appeals to what is most noble in him. His father, Tobit, who sends him on a journey to obtain money for their future (see Tob 4:2), first wants to pass on to him his most important inheritance, what he has valued most in his own life.

> My son, when I die, bury me, and do not neglect your mother. Honor her all the days of your life; do what is pleasing to her, and do not grieve her.… Remember the Lord our God all your days, my son, and refuse to sin or to transgress his commandments.… Do not turn your face away from any poor man, and the face of God will not

8   Msgr. Fernando Ocáriz, *Pastoral Letter*, February 14, 2017, 25.

be turned away from you. If you have many possessions, make your gift from them in proportion; if few, do not be afraid to give according to the little you have.… Bless the Lord God on every occasion; ask him that your ways may be made straight and that all your paths and plans may prosper. (Tob 4:3–19)

Several weeks later Tobias, recently married, is about to begin the return journey to his parents' home, and his new mother-in-law, Edna, makes a parting request: "The Lord of heaven bring you back safely, dear brother, and grant me to see your children by my daughter Sarah, that I may rejoice before the Lord. See, I am entrusting my daughter to you; do nothing to grieve her" (Tob 10:12).

God calls husband and wife to protect one another, to care for one another, to pour out their lives for one another: from here stems the secret of their personal fulfillment, which therefore can never be merely *self*-fulfillment. The deepest meaning of life is to give life. That is what we see in Jesus' life: "I came that they may have life, and have it abundantly" (Jn 10:10). That is also how St. Joseph and Our Lady lived, with the most humble, tender, and refined love this world has ever seen, caring for one another and caring above all for Life made flesh. And that is how God wants his disciples to live, so that wherever we are we radiate his joy, his eagerness for life. This is the nucleus of the meaning of our Christian mission.

The lack of love and smiling has turned our cities into deserts. So much entertainment, so many things for wasting time, for making laughter, but love is lacking. The smile of a family can overcome this desertification of our cities. This is the victory of family love. No economic and political engineering can substitute this contribution of families. The Babel project builds lifeless skyscrapers. The Spirit of God instead makes the desert fruitful (cf. Is 32:15)."[9]

The deepest meaning of life is to give life. This discovery, which can be made even as an adolescent, but which sometimes is only attained late in life, marks the true passage from childhood to human maturity. We could say that only then do we truly begin to be a person: only then does life truly begin. For

having great dreams is the sign of life; loving, this is what life means. Loving to the point of being able to give oneself for the beloved. Being able to forget about oneself, this is to be oneself; being able to die for something, this is to live. A person who only thinks about himself is no one, is empty; only a person who can forget about himself, who can give himself, who can love in a word, is alive.[10]

The Scope of a "Yes"

In this light, we see how far removed the vocation to marriage is from *an impulse to self-satisfaction or a mere means to selfish fulfilment*

---

9   Pope Francis, General Audience (September 2, 2015).
10   Joan Maragall, "Elogio del vivir," in *Vida escrita* (Madrid: Aguilar, 1959), p. 105.

of one's own personality.[11] Certainly, our personality is only truly developed when we are able to give ourselves to another person. The life of marriage is also the source of many satisfactions and joys, but no one fails to see that it also brings with it problems, demands, deceptions. Yet how easy it is to seek to escape from this less attractive face of love.

We can think here of how some marriage celebrations are planned with great care, sparing no expense, doing everything possible to ensure that it will be an unforgettable experience and worthy of the family's social position. But then comes the reality of daily life, the disenchantment that can arise after some months or years when faced with the imperfections of family life—when problems arise, when we see more clearly the spouse's defects, and it becomes difficult to talk with one another, to listen to one another, to heal wounds that are opened, to pour out affection. Then we can begin to lose sight of the fact that marriage is "a real call from God," which asks the spouses to truly give themselves, as a father, a mother, a husband, a wife—with a vocation. And this would truly be unfortunate: a family that God wanted to be happy, even amid difficulties and hardships, and that ends up off the path, content to merely "put up with" one another.

The day a man and a woman are married, they answer "yes" to the question about whether they love one another. But the true answer is only given by their own life: forged in the slow fire of the

11   St. Josemaría, *Christ is Passing By*, 42.

"forever" of their mutual yes. "One always answers the most important questions with one's whole life. It doesn't matter what one says,
the words one uses. In the end, the answer comes from the deeds
of one's life. Who are you? What do you truly want? The answer
comes only from one's entire life."[12] And this yes of one's entire life,
made a reality once and again each day, becomes ever deeper and
more authentic. The unavoidable naiveté that marks the beginning
of married life is transformed into a light-filled innocence, without
any cynicism: into a "yes, dear" that now knows, but also loves.

The immense depth of this yes, irrevocable if love is to be true,
is also the reason the Church continues to go against the current
in her teachings about the engagement period and the openness
of the spouses to life. Although this stance leads to accusations of
being unenlightened and harsh, she insists patiently because she
knows that God is calling her to safeguard the truth of human
love, especially in its "native place."[13] In doing so, the Church is not
defending an abstract truth, a rule from a manual as it were. Rather,
she is protecting the truth of specific lives, of families; she is protecting human relationships from the truly deadly sickness—from
the venom that subtly works its way in, clothed at first as romance
and triumph, until it is suddenly unmasked, perhaps only after a
number of years, as what it really is: the selfishness that can trap
each spouse in themselves.

---

12   Sandor Marai, *El último encuentro* (Barcelona: Salamanca, 2007), p. 107.
13   Msgr. Fernando Ocáriz, *Pastoral Letter*, June 4, 2017.

It's true that there is an apparent magnanimity and joy of living in a person who decides, "I'm going to enjoy all that my body can give me, and share it with whoever wants to join me." In this approach to life, we can hear a clear echo from the first chapters of Genesis: youth is such a savory fruit; why not taste it to the full? Why does God want to deprive me of this sweetness? (see Gen 3:2,6). Young people today who are seeking to lead a Christian life feel this same attraction, but they see that it is only a mirage, and they want to grasp the truth more deeply. By their effort to keep their love pure, or to regain their innocence if perhaps they have lost it, they are preparing themselves to love without "possessing" the other person, without "consuming" them. In one way or another they ask themselves: With whom am I going to share this eagerness for life that I sense inside? Is this really the right person? Are we going to truly love one another, or only desire one another? They know that with their body they are also going to give their heart, their person, their freedom. They know that all this only truly fits within a "yes, forever"; and they know that they and every person are worthy of a "yes, without terms and conditions." If this decision is missing, they are not ready to make this gift, nor are the others ready to receive it; it is a gift that would leave them empty inside, although they might discover this only with the passage of time.

The same "logic" underlies the vocation of those who are celibate and who also want to love God with their body, because they give it to him day after day. Yes, matrimony and celibacy mutually illumine and need one another, because both of them give expression to a gratuitousness that can only be understood in God's light, from the self-image God has placed in us, by which we see ourselves as a gift, we see others as a gift, and we realize we are called to give life: to our parents, children, grandchildren... to everyone.

When Jesus reveals this deep meaning of love, his disciples are perplexed, so much so that he has to tell them: "Not all men can receive this precept, but only those to whom it is given" (Mt 19:11). Young people and parents who are trying to lead a Christian life, although they may at times encounter a lack of understanding in others, should realize that deep down many people admire them, although sometimes they can't express exactly why. They admire them because with their sincere love they are giving clear expression to the joy and freedom of God's love, the desire for which each man and woman harbors deep in their heart, "with sighs too deep for words" (Rom 8:26).

A Heart That Doesn't Want to Suffer

The name Raphael means "God heals." It means God watches over and cares for each person. The archangel's intervention in the lives of Tobit, Anna, Tobias, and Sarah is a visible expression of a reality we may often lose sight of: God's protective care for families, the importance he gives to their success and happiness (see Tob 12:11–15). God wants to be close to us, although we at times refuse to let him, because we don't truly want him to be close. In the story of the prodigal son, who went off to a "far country" (Lk 15:13), we can see not only specific people, but also entire societies and cultures: a world that distances itself from God and thus becomes a hostile place where many families suffer, and sometimes suffer shipwreck. Despite everything, like the father in the parable, God never tires of waiting, and always finds a way to be present in these sometimes-tragic realities, seeking out each person, even when many wounds have to be healed.

The Book of Tobit also shows us how God's closeness to and concern for families does not mean being spared from every difficulty, whether internal or external. Tobit, for example, is a righteous man, even heroic, and yet God allows him to become blind (Tob 2:10). His wife, as a result, has to try to find income for the family, and one day, along with her salary she is given a kid. Tobit, perhaps in a bad mood because of his blindness, thinks his wife has stolen the kid and unintentionally causes a commotion in the family. As Tobit himself tells us: "But I did not believe her, and told her to return it to the owners; and I blushed for her. Then she replied to me, 'Where are your charities and your righteous deeds? You seem to know everything!'" (Tob 2:14). Faced with this harsh response, Tobit is filled with grief and begins to weep and pray, asking God to take him to be with him (Tob 3:1–6).

Nevertheless, Tobit continues doing all he can to make his wife happy, although he isn't always successful. Thus, for example, when Tobias is already on his journey back home, now happily married and with the money his father had asked him to recover, his mother, Anna, who right from the start was opposed to Tobias making the trip, fears the worst: "The lad has perished; his long delay proves it.… Am I not distressed, my child, that I let you go, you who are the light of my eyes?" Tobit, who is also worried, tries to reassure her: "Be still and stop worrying; he is well." And Anna replies, "Be still and stop deceiving me; my child has perished." But with a mother's inconsistent heart, she secretly continues hoping for his return: "And she went out every day to the road by which they had left; she ate nothing in the daytime, and throughout the nights she never stopped mourning for her son Tobias" (Tob 10:1–7).

It is moving to see how, over the centuries, the daily challenges faced by families haven't changed much. Misunderstandings, failures to communicate, worries about the children: *We would have a poor idea of marriage and of human affection if we were to think that love and joy come to an end when faced with such difficulties.*[14] The initial process of falling in love—which provides the strength needed to dream of forming a family—tends to cover over the defects of the other person. But a few weeks of living under the same roof are enough to realize that no one arrives perfect for the wedding day, and that therefore married life needs to be a path of constant conversion for both spouses, working together as a team. As long as husband and wife continue giving one another a new opportunity each day, their hearts will grow each day more beautiful, even though some of their limitations will still remain, and even become crystallized.

14   St. Josemaría, *Christ is Passing By*, 24

An old song says: "A heart that doesn't want to suffer, spends its entire life free of loves."[15] And C. S. Lewis wrote in this regard:

> To love at all is to be vulnerable. Love anything, and your heart will certainly be wrung and possibly be broken. If you want to make sure of keeping it intact, you must give your heart to no one, not even to an animal. Wrap it carefully round with hobbies and little luxuries; avoid all entanglements; lock it up safe in the casket or coffin of your selfishness.[16]

Certainly, newlyweds don't encounter the same danger Tobias and Sarah did, who had to be ready to face the danger of death on their wedding night, through the malice of an evil spirit (see Tob 6:14–15; 7:11). Yet the devil of selfishness—a deadly enemy—constantly threatens all families, with the temptation to "make mountains" out of *the unimportant little frictions that selfishness could magnify out of proportion.*[17]

Hence how important it is for husband and wife to speak clearly, even when this involves broaching difficult topics, and not entrench themselves bit by bit behind a high wall: they need to rebuild, once and again, the sentiments that make love possible. St. Josemaría said that *quarrels, so long as they don't happen often, are also a proof*

---

15   "A los árboles altos," a popular song St. Josemaría alludes to in *The Way*, 145.

16   C. S. Lewis, *The Four Loves*, chap. 6

17   St. Josemaría, *Christ is Passing By*, 23.

of love, and they are almost a need.[18] Water needs to flow freely, since if it becomes stagnant it begins to cover over with algae. Therefore, it is also very important that parents

> *find time to spend with their children, to talk with them. They are the most important thing—more important than business or work or rest. In their conversations, parents should make an effort to listen, to pay attention, to understand, to recognize the fact that their children are sometimes partly right—or even completely right—in some of their rebellious attitudes.*[19]

Above all, husband and wife need to talk with God, asking him to grant them his light: "Thy word is a lamp to my feet and a light to my path" (Ps 119:105). Although the book of Tobit never tells us of any disagreements between Tobias and Sarah, we can easily imagine these taking place, as with those between Tobit and Anna and as with all families. But we can also imagine them closely united right to the end of their lives, because we see their marriage strengthened through intimate union with God. "Blessed art thou, O God of our fathers, and blessed be thy holy and glorious name for ever," Tobias prays on his wedding night. "Grant that I may find mercy and may grow old together with her" (Tob 8:5, 7).

St. John Paul II, "the Pope of the family,"[20] once compared the spousal love in the Song of Songs to the love between Tobias

---

18   St. Josemaría, *Christ is Passing By*, 26.
19   St. Josemaría, *Christ is Passing By*, 27.
20   Pope Francis, Canonization Homily (April 27, 2014).

and Sarah. "The spouses in the Song of Songs, with ardent words, declare to each other their human love. The newlyweds in the book of Tobit ask God that they be able to respond to love."[21] By bringing together these two descriptions of married love, he wanted to raise the question, Which of the two reflects it better?. The answer is easy: both. The day when two hearts find one another, their vocation takes on a fresh and youthful face, like the spouses in the Song. But this face recovers its youthfulness each time that, throughout their lives, the two of them welcome anew their calling *to respond to love*. And then, yes, this love becomes as strong as death.[22]

21   St. John Paul II, General Audience (June 27, 1984).
22   See St. John Paul II, General Audience (June 27, 1984); and Song 8:6.

CHAPTER 8

BEING BETTER MOTHERS AND FATHERS THAN EVER

Diego Zalbidea

The mother of James and John is eager to speak with Jesus. She kneels before him trustingly and says she wants to ask him for something. Jesus replies: "What do you want?" She goes right to the point: "Command that these two sons of mine may sit, one at your right hand and one at your left, in your kingdom" (Mt 20:21). Jesus may have smiled at the boldness of this mother's request. But soon he will grant her sons much more than she could ever have dreamt of. He will give them an abode in his heart and a universal and eternal mission.

The Church, which then was just beginning, is today experiencing a new apostolic impulse. Through the recent Roman pontiffs, our Lord is calling her to an "evangelization ever renewed"[1]—one of the dominant notes in the passage from the second to the third millennium. And the family plays a key role in this adventure. Mothers, fathers, grandparents are the protagonists: they are on the front line of evangelization. For the family "is the first place where the Love of God is made present in our lives, beyond anything we can do or fail to do."[2] In the family we learn how to pray, with words we will continue to use our entire life; in the family the way we look at the world and other people takes shape.[3] The home is called to be the right environment, the good soil where God can plant his seed, so that it may bear fruit and yield "in one case a hundredfold, in another sixty, and in another thirty" (Mt 13:23).

Parents of Saints

St. Josemaría was still a young priest when our Lord showed him the immense panorama of holiness that his work would sow in the world. He realized he could not put off this mission and asked his

---

1   St. Paul VI, Apostolic Exhortation *Evangelii Nuntiandi* (December 8, 1975), 82. See also St. John Paul II, Apostolic Letter at the Close of the Great Jubilee of the Year 2000 *Novo Millennio Ineunte* (January 6, 2001), 40; Benedict XVI, Homily at the Opening of the Synod of Bishops on the New Evangelization (October 7, 2012); Francis, Apostolic Exhortation on the Proclamation of the Gospel *Evangelii Gaudium* (November 24, 2013), 27.

2   Msgr. Fernando Ocáriz, *Letter*, June 4, 2017.

3   See the *Catechism of the Catholic Church*, 1655–1666.

spiritual director to let him undertake more prayer and penance. To justify these requests, he wrote to him saying, *Look, God is asking me for this, and besides I need to be a saint and father, a teacher and guide of saints.*[4] We could apply these words, in some way, to any mother or father of a family, since sanctity is authentic only if it is shared and gives light to those nearby. Therefore, if we aspire to true sanctity, each of us is called to be "a saint and father, a teacher and guide of saints."

From very early on, St. Josemaría spoke about a *vocation for marriage.*[5] He knew this expression would surprise many people, but he was convinced that marriage is a true path to sanctity, and that conjugal love is very close to God's heart. Using a striking phrase he said, *I bless this love with my two hands, and if anyone asks me why I say with my two hands, I reply at once: Because I don't have four!*[6]

The mission of parents is not limited to welcoming the children God gives them. It lasts their whole life, and has as its goal heaven. Although at times the affection of parents for their children can seem fragile and imperfect, the bond of fatherhood and motherhood is in fact so deeply rooted that it makes possible a self-giving without limits: any mother would gladly take the place of a suffering child of hers in a hospital bed.

Sacred Scripture is replete with mothers and fathers who feel privileged and proud of the children God has given them: Abraham

4   St. Josemaría, *Intimate notes*, 1752.

5   St. Josemaría, *The Way*, 27.

6   St. Josemaría, *Friends of God*, 184.

and Sarah; the mother of Moses; Hannah, the mother of Samuel; the mother of the seven Maccabean brothers; the Canaanite woman who beseeches Jesus for her daughter; the widow at Nain; Elizabeth and Zachary; and, very especially, Our Lady and St. Joseph. These are intercessors to whom we can entrust our families, so that they may be protagonists in a new generation of holy men and women.

We are well aware that motherhood and fatherhood are intimately tied to the Cross and suffering. Along with great joys and satisfactions, the process of children growing up and maturing entails many difficulties, some smaller and others not so small: nights without sleep, the rebellions of adolescence, difficulties in finding work, finding the right person to share their life with, and many others.

Especially painful is seeing how at times children make bad decisions or distance themselves from the Church. The parents have truly tried to raise them in the faith; they have endeavored to show them how attractive the Christian life is. And so they may ask themselves, What have we done wrong? It's not surprising that this question may arise, although they shouldn't let themselves be tormented by it. It's true that parents bear the main responsibility for educating their children, but they aren't the only ones who influence them. The surrounding environment often presents children with other outlooks on life that seem more attractive and convincing, or that make the world of faith seem distant and unreal. And above all, children have their own freedom to decide which path they want to follow.

Sometimes it's simply the case that children need to distance themselves for a while, so as to rediscover with new appreciation what they have received from their parents. When this happens, parents need to be patient. Although their children have taken a mistaken path, they still need to truly accept them, make their love known to them, and avoid any undue pressure, which could end up driving them even further way. "Often there is nothing else to do but wait; pray and wait with patience, gentleness, magnanimity and mercy."[7] The example of the father in the parable of the prodigal son is very instructive in this regard (Lk 15:11–32). Although he was well aware of the mistakes his son had made, he also realized he had to wait.

In any case, it isn't always easy for a mother or father to accept the freedom of their children when they start growing up—even when decisions are good in themselves, they may be different than what the parents would like. Parents can even begin to see themselves as simply spectators of the lives of their children, who up to now have needed them for almost everything. Nevertheless, even though it might seem paradoxical, this is when children need their parents more than ever. The same people who taught them how to eat and walk can continue accompanying the growth of their freedom as they open up their own path in life. The parents are now called to be teachers and guides.

---

7   Pope Francis, General Audience (February 4, 2015).

Teachers of Saints

Parents are truly teachers, often without realizing it. Almost by osmosis, they pass on to their children so many things that will stay with them their whole lives. And they have to educate them especially in the most important art: learning how to love and be loved. Here one of the most difficult lessons is the true meaning of freedom.

To begin with, parents need to help them overcome some prejudices that today might seem beyond dispute, such as the view that freedom means "acting in accord with one's caprices and without restraint by any law."[8] Nevertheless, the true challenge they have before them is to awaken in their children, with patience and perseverance, a liking for doing the good that strengthens bit by bit. Then children won't see only the difficulties involved in doing what their parents tell them, but they will develop the capacity to "rejoice in the good."[9] Along this path of growth, children will sometimes fail to appreciate all that their parents teach them. And it's true that often the parents also need to learn how to educate their children better: a person isn't born knowing how to be a father or mother. Nevertheless, despite possible mistakes in how they are raised, children over time will come to have a deeper appreciation for what they have been taught at home. As St. Josemaría said with

---

8   Msgr. Fernando Ocáriz, *Letter*, 9 January 2018, 5.
9   *Reaching the Entire Person, Role of the Emotions (I)*. Available at *opusdei.org*.

regard to some advice his mother once gave him: *Many years later I came to see how wise those words were.*[10]

Children end up discovering, sooner or later, how much their parents have loved them and how well they have taught them the keys to life. The epilogue to Dostoevsky's great novel *The Brothers Karamazov* expresses this eloquently:

> There is nothing higher and stronger and more wholesome and good for life in the future than some good memory, especially a memory of childhood, of home. People talk to you a great deal about your education, but some good, sacred memory, preserved from childhood, is perhaps the best education. If a man carries many such memories with him into life, he is safe to the end of his days, and if one has only one good memory left in one's heart, even that may sometime be the means of saving us.

Parents know that their mission is to sow and wait patiently for their diligent efforts to bear fruit, although they may never see all of the good results.

Guides of Saints

A guide is someone who leads and teaches others to follow or open up a path. To do so they need to know the terrain very well and accompany those who travel it for the first time. Good guides and teachers shape both the head and the heart. Salome, the wife of

10   St. Josemaría, Notes from a Family Gathering, February 17, 1958.

Zebedee, accompanied her sons along Christ's path and was present at the foot of the Cross. Only John joined her there, but James would end up being the first apostle to give his life for Jesus. She was also present at the tomb on Sunday morning, along with Mary Magdalene. And John followed her there soon afterwards.

Every guide sometimes needs to confront a complicated and challenging journey. In the journey of life, one of these is the path of replying to God's call. Accompanying their children in discerning their vocation is an important part of parents' own mission. It's easy to understand why they may confront this challenging step with fear. St. Josemaría told a group of young people: *Fear? Some words of St. John, from his first letter, in chapter 4, are engraved on my heart:* Qui autem timet, non est perfectus in caritate *(1 Jn 4:18). A person who is afraid doesn't know how to love. And all of you know how to love, so you have no fear. Fear of what? You know how to love; therefore you have no fear. Forward!*[11]

Certainly, the biggest concern of a mother or father is the happiness of their children. But often they may have formed an idea of what path that happiness should take. Sometimes parents dream of a professional future that fails to match their children's real talents. Or they may hope that their children will be good, but "without overdoing things." Perhaps they have forgotten the radical, and at times disconcerting, parts of the Gospel message. Therefore, and with even more reason if they have received a deeply

11   St. Josemaría, Notes from a Get-Together with Young People, November 1972.

Christian upbringing, it is inevitable that "each child will surprise us with ideas and projects born of that freedom, which challenge us to rethink our own ideas. This is a good thing. Education includes encouraging the responsible use of freedom."[12]

Parents know their children very well—usually, better than anyone. And since they want the best for them, it's only natural and right that they are concerned that their choices in life will make them happy, and that they consider their children's future with a view to their human prosperity, and seek to protect and help them.[13] Therefore when their children begin to discern a possible call from God, parents are faced with the beautiful role of being a prudent guide. When St. Josemaría spoke about his vocation to his father, the latter told his son: "Think it over a bit more." But right away he added, "I won't place obstacles."[14] Therefore, while trying to give realistic and sensible advice regarding their children's spiritual decisions, parents need to learn to respect their freedom and detect the

12 Pope Francis, Apostolic Exhortation on Love in the Family *Amoris Laetitia* (March 19, 2016), 262. St. Josemaría spoke about this concern in a humorous way: "No sooner is the child born but Mom is already planning to have him married to a particular girl, and they'll do this or that. Dad thinks about the boy's career or about getting him involved in the business. Each one composes a novel, a wonderful romantic novel. Afterwards, the boy grows up bright, turns out well, because his parents are good, and then says to them: That novel of yours is not to my liking. And we have a fine pair of tantrums" (Notes from a Get-Together with Families, November 4, 1972).

13 The idiomatic expression used by St. Josemaría here is "de tejas abajo," "in light of this world's concerns." See Javier Echevarría, *Memoria del Beato Josemaría Escrivá* (Madrid: Rialp, 2000), p. 99.

14 Ana Sastre, *Tiempo de caminar* (Madrid: Rialp,1989), p. 52.

action of God's grace in their hearts, so as not to become—whether wanting to do so or not—an obstacle to God's plans.

Moreover, children often fail to realize what a strong "shock" their vocation can be for their parents. St. Josemaría said that the only time he saw his father cry was when he told him he wanted to be a priest.[15] A lot of generosity is required from parents to accompany their children on a path in life that is different from what they were hoping for. So it's not surprising that it is hard for them to renounce these plans. But God is not asking less of the parents than he is of their children: this suffering, which is very human, can also be, with God's grace, very divine.

These shocks can also be moments to consider, as St. Josemaría used to say, that children owe to their parents 90 percent of their call to love God with an undivided heart.[16] God is well aware of the sacrifice it can require of parents to accept this decision with affection and freedom. He who gave his own Son to save us understands this better than anyone.

When parents generously accept the call of their children by God, without holding on to them for themselves, they draw down abundant blessings from heaven for many people. Down through the centuries this has often taken place. When Jesus called John and James to follow him and leave everything, they were helping their father to mend the nets. Zebedee continued working on the

15   See Andrés Vázquez de Prada, *The Founder of Opus Dei*, vol. 1, p. 73.
16   See St. Josemaría, *Conversations*, 104.

nets, perhaps a bit upset, but he let them leave. It probably took him some time to realize that it was God himself who was entering his family. But in the end, how great would be his joy to see his sons happy in this new "fishing" enterprise, in the "sea without shores" of the apostolate.

More Needed than Ever

When a daughter or son makes an important decision for their life, the parents are more needed than ever. A mother or father can often discern, even from afar, traces of sadness in their children, as they can also sense authentic joy. Therefore, they can have an irreplaceable role in helping them to be happy and faithful.

To carry out this new role, perhaps the first thing they need to do is to recognize the gift they have received. By considering this in God's presence, they will come to realize that *it is no "sacrifice" for parents when God asks them for their children. Neither, for those He calls, is it a sacrifice to follow Him. It is, on the contrary, an immense honor, a motive for a great and holy pride, a mark of predilection, a very special affection that God has shown.*[17] They are the ones who have made possible this vocation, which is a continuation of the gift of life. Therefore St. Josemaría used to tell parents: *I congratulate you, because Jesus has taken these pieces of your heart—totally—for Himself alone… for Himself alone!*[18]

17   St. Josemaría, *The Forge*, 18.
18   Words of St. Josemaría when meeting with some families, October 22, 1960.

The parents' prayer then takes on great importance in our Lord's eyes. We can find many examples of this marvelous intercession in the Bible and in history. St. Monica's trusting and insistent prayer for the conversion of her son Augustine is perhaps the best known, but in reality, there are countless examples. Behind every vocation "there is always the strong and intense prayer of someone: a grand-mother, a grandfather, a mother, a father, a community… Vocations are born in prayer and from prayer; and only through prayer can they persevere and bear fruit."[19] Once the path of a vocation has been undertaken, following it to the end depends in good measure on the prayer of those who love that person most.

Along with prayer, parents need to stay close to their child. Seeing their parents take an interest in their new mission in life helps greatly to strengthen the children's fidelity. Often parents have a great desire, without saying so expressly, to help out and share in the happiness of their daughter or son on this path of self-giving. They need to experience the fruitfulness of their lives. Sometimes it will be the children who ask them in a winning way for advice, help, or prayer. How many stories there are of fathers and mothers who discover their calling to sanctity through the vocation of their children!

The fruit of James' and John's self-giving is immeasurable. But we can be sure that these two pillars of the Church owe to their mother and father the biggest part of their vocation. James

19   Pope Francis, *Regina Caeli* (April 21, 2013).

brought the love of God to the very ends of the known world, and John proclaimed it with words that are among the most beautiful ever written about this love. All of us who have received the faith thanks to their self-giving should feel a deep gratitude towards this married couple from the shores of the Sea of Galilee. The names of Zebedee and Salome will be repeated, with those of the apostles, until the end of time.

"Take this, all of you, and eat of it, for this is my Body, which will be given up for you."[20] Mothers and fathers who truly love God, and who have seen how a child of theirs has given himself or herself to him completely, enjoy a very special understanding of our Lord's words in the consecration at Mass. In some way they experience them in their own lives. They have given their child so that others may have nourishment and life. Thus, their children somehow "multiply" their own motherhood and fatherhood. By giving this new "yes," they unite themselves to the work of the Redemption, which culminates in Christ's "yes" in the Passion, and which began, in a humble home, in the "yes" of Mary.

20 *Roman Missal*, Eucharistic Prayer.

CHAPTER 9

OUR WE MAKING THE RIGHT DECISION?

Pablo Marti

The apostles are thoughtful as they reflect on Jesus' recent encounter with the rich young man, and how it had ended: the young man "went away sorrowful" (Mt 19:22). They may be disconcerted at how Jesus had looked at him, not sorrowfully but yes with hurt in his eyes: "it will be hard for a rich man to enter the kingdom of heaven" (Mt 19:23). As on other occasions, Peter makes himself the spokesman for their shared concern: "Lo, we have left everything and followed you. What then shall we have?" (Mt 19:27) Echoing these words, and with the same familiarity of a good friend, St. Josemaría addressed our Lord in a particularly difficult moment in his apostolic work: *What will become of us?…*

What are you going to do with us now? You can't abandon those who have placed their trust in You![1]

What Will Become of Me?

The beginning of a vocation, like the start of any path, usually brings with it an element of uncertainty. When God allows unrest to enter our heart, and we begin to sense that a specific path might be the right one for us, it's only natural that we ask ourselves, Is this the right way?

What lies behind this doubt? First of all, this fear—fear about our life and our own decisions—is quite normal. We don't know what the future will bring, where this path is leading us, because we have never traveled it before. This doubt is also a sign of our desire to make the right decision; we want our life to be of value, to leave a mark. Moreover, any great and beautiful endeavor demands the best of us, and we don't want to rush into things. But the deepest reason is both more mysterious and simpler at the same time: God is seeking us, and we want to live with him. Usually, it is not God we are afraid of, but our own selves. Our own fragility in the face of such an immense love unsettles us; we think we can never measure up to it.

When Peter asks Jesus "what will become of us"; when St. Josemaría asks Jesus "what will become of us"; when a Christian asks Jesus "what will become of me" if I set out on this path; how

---

1   Andrés Vázquez de Prada, *The Founder of Opus Dei*, vol. 3 (Scepter), pp. 27–28.

does Christ respond? Jesus speaks right to our heart, his voice brimming with joy and affection. He tells us that each of us is a wager on God's part, and that God never loses his bets. Life entails adventure, risk, limitations, challenges, effort; it requires letting go of the small world we can control and discovering the beauty of dedicating our life to something greater than ourselves, which fully satisfies our hunger for happiness. We can imagine the keen look in Jesus' eyes when he speaks those words that have resounded and will continue to resound in many hearts: "every one who has left houses or brothers or sisters or father or mother or children or lands, for my name's sake, will receive a hundredfold, and inherit eternal life" (Mt 19:29). God never gives in half measures.

Nevertheless, we can't expect to receive a crystal-clear revelation, or a plan spelled out down to the last detail. God has a plan in mind for us, but he also counts on our own initiative.

When a person is uncertain of a special call from God, one needs to ask the Holy Spirit for "light to see" one's vocation. But if the person concerned and those whose role it is to help in the discerning of a vocation (for example, through spiritual direction) see no objective impediment, and if Providence (ordinarily through human channels) has actually guided that person towards that experience, then in addition to continuing to ask for "light to see," it is important (a first priority, I would say) to ask the Holy Spirit for "strength to want to," so that by that strength which lifts up freedom in time, the divine and eternal vocation itself may take shape.[2]

We Are Not Alone: The Church Accompanies Us

In the process of discerning our own vocation we are never alone, since every vocation is born and takes shape in the Church. Through our Mother the Church, God attracts us toward himself and calls us, and the Church herself welcomes and accompanies us on our path towards God.

The Church Attracts

In the course of history, God makes use of people who open a deep furrow with their life, who mark out paths for the self-giving of others. Their life, their ideals, their teachings inspire and unsettle us; they draw us out of our selfishness and call us to a fuller life, a life of love. This call forms part of God's plans—of the action of the Holy Spirit who prepares the way for us.

The Church Calls

God *doesn't ask our permission to "complicate" our lives. He just gets in…and that's that!*[3] And to do so, he relies on his children's daring in inviting others to seriously consider the possibility of dedicating their life to him. Jesus compared the kingdom of heaven to a great

---

2   Msgr. Fernando Ocáriz, "Vocation to Opus Dei as a Vocation in the Church," in *Opus Dei in the Church* (Four Courts Press—Scepter, 1994), p. 89.

3   St. Josemaría, *The Forge*, 902.

banquet that God wants all men and women to take part in, including those who initially didn't seem to be invited (see Lk 14:15–24). And in fact, God usually relies on an *external invitation* to make his voice resound in a person's heart.

Every vocation in the Church, when it meets with a loving response, leads to sanctity. Therefore, the best vocation for each person is his or her own. But no paths are closed "a priori." A life leading toward God in marriage or in celibacy is in principle open to everyone. Our biography, our personal history, gradually shapes our own path and places before us specific choices. The choice depends on our personal freedom: it is just that, a choice. Christ wants us to be free: "if any man would come after me…" (Mt 16:24); "if you would be perfect…" (Mt 19:21).

But what leads a person to choose a specific vocation among all the possible ones? Our freedom seeks great horizons, divine horizons of love. St. Ignatius of Antioch said: "Christianity is not a matter of persuasive words, but of greatness,"[4] the greatness that is Christ's love. It is enough to set forth a specific path in the Church in all its beauty and simplicity, through our life and words, for souls to be drawn to it by its own force, provided they let themselves be challenged by Christ (see Mk 10:21). Something in the person's own heart—very intimate and deep and mysterious, even for that person—resonates in harmony with this proposal of a path within

---

4   St. Ignatius of Antioch, *Letter to the Romans*, 3.

the Church. As the Greek philosopher said: like is known by like.[5] The authentic life of other Christians calls us to draw close to Jesus and give him our heart. We see an example of sanctity in people close to us and we think: "Perhaps I too...". It is the "come and see" of the Gospel, which challenges us here and now (Jn 1:46).

The Church Welcomes and Accompanies

Any normal person, even without experiencing a special call, can set out on a life of service and self-giving: in celibacy or in matrimony, in the priesthood, in the religious state. The discernment of each person's vocation involves looking at the right intention and abilities of that person, his or her suitability for a specific path.

This discernment requires the help of other people, especially through spiritual direction. Moreover, it also requires the deliberation of those who govern the specific institution in the Church that is being considered as a possible path in life. The mission of welcoming, on the part of the Church, also involves making certain that each of us finds our right place. If we reflect on it, clearly it is a divine blessing that, when trying to decide on the plan for our life, we find people in whom we can trust and who in turn trust us. Thus, other people, with a deep knowledge of our personal situation, can state in conscience: "take heart, you can do it, you have the required conditions and talent for this mission, which may be for

5   Aristotle, *De Anima* I, 2.

you and which you can accept, if you truly want to"; or who can tell us, also in conscience: "perhaps this isn't your path."

A vocation is always a "win-win" situation. It is the best for each of the two sides of the relationship: the person in question and the Church institution involved. Our Father God follows each of these personal histories very closely with his loving providence. The Holy Spirit has raised up in the Church institutions and paths of holiness that can be channels and help for specific people. And it is also the Holy Spirit who urges individuals, at a specific moment in their life, to enrich with their own self-giving these channels in the Church.

A Leap of Faith: Trusting in God

Seeing the multitude of people following him, Jesus asks Philip: "How are we to buy bread, so that these people may eat?" (Jn 6:5). The apostles realize very clearly that they can do nothing to provide for the hunger of so many people. They have only "five barley loaves and two fish," brought by a young boy. Jesus, taking the loaves, provides food for everyone, and so much is left over that he tells the disciples: "Gather up the fragments left over, that nothing may be lost" (Jn 6:12). Only Jesus can ensure that nothing in our life is lost, that it is of service to all mankind; but we have to entrust all that we have to him. Then he works miracles, and we are the first to benefit.

Trusting in God, opening to him the doors of our life, leads us to have compassion on the multitude that is hungering for him, like sheep without a shepherd. And it leads us to realize that he is relying on us to bring his love to all these people. And then, to set out, because it is an endeavor we could never have conceived of on our own account—to set out, realizing that with God's help we will go forward: placing ourselves in his hands, relying totally on him. And since God does not impose himself on us, a "leap of faith" is needed: *"Why don't you give yourself to God once and for all… really… now!"*

Certainly, one needs to consider things carefully. This is what the Church terms a period of discernment. But it is good to keep in mind that "discernment is not a solipsistic self-analysis or a form of egotistical introspection, but an authentic process of leaving ourselves behind in order to approach the mystery of God, who helps us to carry out the mission to which he has called us, for the good of our brothers and sisters."[6] Vocation implies getting out of ourselves, leaving behind our comfort zone and personal security.

If we decide to make a parachute jump, the parachute needs to open properly, so we can land gently. But first we need to leap from the plane with the parachute still shut. In a similar way, vocation requires trusting in God and letting go of our personal supports. St. John Chrysostom said, referring to the Three Wise Men: "While the Magi were in Persia, they saw only a star. But when they left their homes behind, they saw the Sun of Justice. We can say that

---

6   Pope Francis, Apostolic Exhortation on the Call to Holiness *Gaudete et Exsultate* (March 19, 2018), 175.

they would not have continued to see the star if they had remained in their own country."[7]

You know that your way is not clear, and that by not following Jesus closely you remain with that clouded vision. Then, what are you waiting for to make up your mind?[8] I can follow a path only if I choose it and live what I have chosen. To continue seeing the star, we need to set out, because God's plans always exceed our own capabilities. It is only by trusting in him that we become capable. At the beginning we can't do it, and we need to grow. But to grow we need to believe: "apart from me you can do nothing" (Jn 15:5)—but with him you can do everything.

Hence, the mistake of those who spend their youth waiting for a definitive illumination of their path in life, and fail to make a decision. Nowadays there is also a special obstacle: so many selfies are taken, young people see themselves in so many photos, that they could even begin to think they already know themselves perfectly. Nevertheless, to truly find one's own identity one needs to rediscover *what one doesn't yet see* about one's own life: its element of "mystery," God's presence and his love for each person. Living fully means discovering and abandoning oneself trustingly to this mystery, accepting a logic and way of reasoning that we cannot fully grasp.

The histories written by God begin little by little. But a trust that risks everything is the path to achieving our greatest dreams,

7   St. John Chrysostom, *Homilies on St. Matthew*, VII, 5.
8   St. Josemaría, *The Way*, 797.

the dreams of God. When, as good children of God, we let ourselves be guided by the Holy Spirit (Rom 8:14), our life attains heights we could never have dreamed of. This is the path of the Magi; of Mary, a young girl who becomes the Mother of God; of Joseph, a carpenter whom God adopts as his father; of the apostles, who rise above their initial mistakes and doubts to become the columns on which the Church is built; and of so many Christians who precede and accompany us. Who could ever have dreamed of this mystery at the beginning of their life? It is only seen clearly at the end. But the ending is possible only because at the beginning each one chose to leave behind their false security and to "leap" into the strong arms of their Father God.[9]

Thus, when discernment has taken place, and a specific vocation has been clarified with definite features, the need becomes clear, in order to continue advancing, for the initial leap of faith: saying "yes." The process of discernment still requires a final stage, and therefore the Church has foreseen, with a wisdom formed by many centuries of experience, the need for a series of progressive steps, to be as certain as possible about the suitability of those who want to take a specific vocational path. This way of acting brings a lot of peace to our heart and strengthens the decision to trust in God, who led us to a path of self-giving. This isn't a question of doubting God but of doubting ourselves, and therefore we trust in him and in the Church.

---

9   See St. Josemaría, *The Way of the Cross*, Seventh Station.

On our part, we need to consider all that we are and have, so as to be able to offer everything, as we see in the parable of the talents (Mt 25:14–30). We can't keep back anything for ourselves and fail to invest it, to share it. This is the key for a mature and sincere decision: the readiness to give everything, to abandon ourselves completely in God's hands, without keeping back anything for ourselves, along with the realization that this self-giving of ours brings a peace and joy that doesn't stem from ourselves. And then the strong conviction begins to take shape that we have truly found our path.

In discerning her vocation, Mary asks the angel: "How can this be, since I have no husband?" (Lk 1:34). The angel is the messenger, the mediator whose call echoes God's voice. Mary places no conditions, but she asks a question in order to be certain. And the angel assures her: the Holy Spirit will act, because what I have told you transcends your understanding, but "with God nothing will be impossible" (Lk 1:37). If even our mother Mary needs to ask, it isn't surprising that each of us needs to ask for advice when we begin to sense God's love in our heart. What should I do to give him my life? What do you think the best path is for me to find happiness? How great it is to seek advice in order to be able to say yes, with a radiant freedom and filled with trust in God. We place our entire being in his hands: "let it be to me according to your word" (Lk 1:38).

PART III
FIDELITY

CHAPTER 10

WE ARE APOSTLES!

José Manuel Antuña

The apostolic adventure inaugurated by Jesus in the world began in Capernaum. We know that at least four of the twelve apostles were fishermen from that town. *When Our Lord called the first Apostles they were busy mending their broken nets by the side of an old boat. Our Lord told them to follow him and* statim, *immediately—they left everything—*relictis omnibus—*everything! And followed him....*[1]

Jesus' words when calling the first apostles marked out a path that will forever change the course of history: "Follow me and I will make you become fishers of men" (Mk 1:17). He doesn't go into more detail. They will continue being fishermen, but from now on they will catch another type of "fish." And they will come to know different "seas," but the skills they have learned in their

1   St. Josemaría, *The Forge*, 356.

work will still be useful. Days of favorable winds and an abundant catch will come, but also slow days, without any fish, or with such a small catch that they will return to shore with the sensation of being empty-handed. But the decisive thing is not the number of fish, or what men judge to be a success or failure; the important thing is what they are going to be. Right from the beginning, Jesus wants them to be aware of their new identity, since he is calling them not only *to do something*—a beautiful and extraordinary undertaking—but *to be someone* who carries out a mission: being "fishers of men."

"All for the Sake of the Gospel"

In responding to God's call, our identity is reconfigured. *It is a new outlook on life*, St. Josemaría said. Realizing that Jesus himself is inviting us to share in his mission enkindles in each person the desire *to dedicate their noblest energies to an activity that, over time, becomes a way of life.* Thus, little by little, *vocation leads us, without realizing it, to take a position in life that we preserve eagerly and joyfully right to the moment of death. And it gives our work a sense of mission.*[2] Over time, it shapes our way of being and acting and of looking at the world, and makes us happy.

As Monsignor Ocáriz said forcefully, "we do not 'do apostolate,' we are apostles!"[3] The apostolic mission doesn't occupy a specific

2   St. Josemaría, *Letter*, January 9, 1932, 9.
3   Msgr. Fernando Ocáriz, *Letter*, February 14, 2017, 9.

time or place in our personal life; rather it affects everything we do and reaches every corner of our life. St. Josemaría insisted right from the beginning to the people in the Work: *Do not forget, my sons, that we are not souls who have joined with other souls to do a good thing. That is a lot... and yet it is little. We are apostles who fulfil* an imperative command from Christ.[4]

"Woe to me if I do not preach the gospel!" St. Paul exclaimed. It was a conviction that he bore deep in his soul. This loving impulse was both an invitation and a duty for him: "if I preach the gospel, that gives me no ground for boasting. For necessity is laid upon me." Hence the only reward he seeks is "that in my preaching I may make the gospel free of charge," since he sees himself as "a slave to all, that I might win the more." Paul opens his heart to us: he is the last of the apostles, unworthy and without merits, but he *is* an apostle. Hence there is no circumstance that is not apostolic for him: "I do it all for the sake of the gospel" (1 Cor 9:16, 18-19, 23). This is his "letter of introduction," and how he wants to be seen: "Paul, a servant of Jesus Christ, called to be an apostle, set apart for the gospel of God" (Rom 1:1).

In a similar way, apostolate for a Christian is not simply a "task" or an activity that takes up certain hours every day, nor even something important that needs to be done. It is a need that stems from a heart that has become "one body, one spirit in Christ,"[5] in union

---

4   St. Josemaría, *Instruction*, March 19, 1934, 27 (emphasis in the original), cited in *The Way: A Critical-historical Edition*, note to 942.

5   *Roman Missal*, Eucharistic Prayer III.

with the whole Church. Being an apostle "is not and cannot be honorary. It involves concretely and even dramatically the entire life of the person concerned."[6] At times we will need the encouragement and advice of other people in our efforts to make Christ known. But since we know our calling is a gift from God, we should ask him that the apostolate flow from our heart as naturally as water from a fountain (see Jn 4:14).

Salt, Light, and Leaven for the World

Our Lord often made use of parables to explain to his disciples the role they were going to carry out in the world. "You are the salt of the earth.… You are the light of the world" (Mt 5:13–14). On another occasion, Jesus spoke to them about leaven—about how a small amount leavens the whole batch (Mt 13:33). For that is how Jesus' apostles have to be: salt that brings joy, light that helps guide others, leaven that makes the whole mass rise. And that is how St. Josemaría envisioned the apostolate of his daughters and sons: *You have a call from God to a specific path: to place yourselves at all the crossroads of the world, with your heart placed in God. And to be there leaven, salt, light for the world. In order to illumine, to give savor, to leaven, to raise up.*[7]

The faithful of Opus Dei, like so many other ordinary Christians, carry out their apostolate in the middle of the world, with

---

6   Pope Benedict XVI, General Audience (September 10, 2008).

7   St. Josemaría, Notes from a Meditation, April 1955, in *Obras* 1956, XI, p. 9.

naturalness and discretion. Although this may sometimes have given rise to misunderstandings, what they are trying to do is simply to make these parables of our Lord a reality in their own lives. Salt isn't seen, when mixed in well with the meal; it gives flavor to food that might otherwise be insipid, even though of good quality. The same is true of leaven: It gives bulk to the bread, without being noticed. The light, in turn, is placed "on a stand, and it gives light to all in the house. Let your light so shine before men" (Mt 5:15–16). It doesn't call attention to itself, however, but to what it seeks to illumine. Christians should enjoy being with others, sharing in their dreams and plans. *We, who are salt and light of Christ, ought to feel uncomfortable when we are not surrounded by people.*[8] This openness, moreover, means interacting with those who don't think like we do, with the serene desire to leave in their hearts the "mark of God."[9] We will do so in the way the Holy Spirit suggests to us: at times saying a short prayer for them; other times, with a friendly word or gesture.

The apostolic effectiveness of a person's life can't be reduced to numbers. Much of the fruit remains hidden, and we will never know about it in this life. But on our part, we need to foster the desire, ever renewed, to live closely united to our Lord. *We Catholics have to go through life being apostles, with God's light and God's salt. We should have no fear, and we should be quite natural; but with so*

8   St. Josemaría, *Alone with God*, 273.
9   See Bishop Javier Echevarría, Homily, September 5, 2010 (*Romana,* 51, July–December 2010).

deep an interior life and such close union with Our Lord that we may shine out, preserving ourselves from corruption and from darkness.[10] God himself will make our efforts fruitful, and we won't waste time worrying about our own shortcomings or external difficulties: that people don't seem to understand us, that they have begun to criticize us, that the path is tiring, that the lake is too big, that I can't make headway in this storm.

Self-Starters

When we consider once again the list of the twelve apostles, we realize how different they were from each other, with quite distinctive personalities. The same is true when we think about the men and women who have been canonized by the Church; and also when we consider the lives of so many ordinary people who follow our Lord with a discrete but determined self-giving. All of them are different, and at the same time, all of them are apostles—faithful, in love with our Lord.

In giving ourselves to God, we don't lose our own personal gifts and qualities; on the contrary, since

> when the Lord thinks of each of you and what he wants to give you, he sees you as his close friend. And if he plans to grant you a grace… it will surely be a gift that will bring you more joy and excitement than anything else in this world. Not because that gift will be rare or extraordinary,

but because it will perfectly fit you. It will be a perfect fit for your entire life.[11]

Hence those who decide to follow our Lord realize, as the years go by, that grace, accompanied by their personal efforts, transforms even their character, making it easier for them to love and serve all men and women. This isn't the result of willpower and striving for an ideal of perfection. Rather, it is the result of Christ's love in an apostle's life.

Soon after his election as prelate, Msgr. Javier Echevarría was asked if he had had a personal life alongside the Founder and his first successor: "Have you been able to be yourself?" His answer is quite moving, reflecting the viewpoint of someone who looks back at his life and sees all that God has done there:

Yes, I certainly have lived my own life. I would never have dreamed of such a fulfilled life as I have had. On my own, my horizons and goals would have been much narrower.… I, as a man of my time, as a Christian and priest, have had a very rich personal life. And my heart is open to the whole world, thanks to having lived alongside two men [St. Josemaría and Bl. Alvaro] with such a big Christian heart.[12]

11 Pope Francis, Apostolic Exhortation to Young People *Christus Vivit* (March 25, 2019), 288.

12 Interview by Pilar Urbano with Bishop Javier Echevarría, *Época*, April 4, 1994, cited in Alvaro Sánchez León, *En la tierra como en el cielo* (Madrid: Rialp, 2019), pp. 349–350.

A person who is sent by Christ and who lets him set the course for their life should never forget that he expects a response that is *deeply free*: Free, in the first place, from selfishness, from pride and the desire to stand out. But free also to place at his service all our talents, initiative, and creativity.

But this spirit of freedom doesn't mean "acting in accord with one's caprices and without restraint by any law,"[13] as though everything that doesn't come from ourselves were an imposition we had to free ourselves from. Rather, it means acting with the same Spirit as Jesus: "I have come down from heaven, not to do my own will, but the will of him who sent me" (Jn 6:38). If apostolate were viewed as simply another "activity," there would be the risk of feeling restricted by the indications of those who coordinate the apostolic initiatives. In contrast, a person who realizes they have been sent by Christ is grateful for the help and impulse that God provides through his many instruments. Living with freedom of spirit means letting the Holy Spirit be the one who shapes and guides us, and who also makes use of those he has placed at our side.

Freedom of spirit leads to us to be "self-starters" when facing challenges in the apostolic mission: that is, doing so not with a passive attitude, but with the conviction that this challenge is what God is asking from us right now and what corresponds to the apostle who we are. Thus, continually, in the small circumstances of our daily life, we can sense the "fresh breeze" of the Spirit, who

13   Msgr. Fernando Ocáriz, *Letter*, January 9, 2018, 5.

impels us to set out "into the deep" (Lk 5:4), in order to continue with him the marvelous history of God's love for us.

If our mission were to "do apostolate," we could be tempted to set it aside when faced with an absorbing work project or an illness, or to take apostolic "vacations." But "we are apostles!" It is our life! Therefore, it would make no sense to head out into the street and leave at home our eagerness to evangelize. Certainly, the apostolic mission will often require an effort, and courage to overcome our fears. Nevertheless, this interior resistance shouldn't unsettle us, since the Holy Spirit fosters in the hearts of those who are docile to him an authentic apostolic spontaneity and creativity, where everything in our life becomes an opportunity for apostolate.

We acquire the *awareness of being on guard duty at an outpost*,[14] in a constant *vigil of love, remaining awake and alert, working diligently*.[15] It is a *vigil of love*, so we shouldn't become anxious or nervous. We have in our hands a marvelous mission that makes us happy and brings happiness to those around us. We are working in the Lord's vineyard and are certain that the undertaking is his. So, if we ever sense a lack of peace in our soul, an excessive tension, then is the moment to draw close to him and say: I am doing this for you; help me to work calmly, with the certainty that you will do everything.

14   St. Josemaría, *Letter*, May 31, 1954, 16.
15   St. Josemaría, *Letter*, May 31, 1954, 16.

Divine Light That Gives Warmth

In the parable of those invited to the wedding feast, when the father learns that some of the invited guests have sent excuses for not coming, he orders his servant to bring in "the poor and maimed and blind and lame" (Lk 14:21). The banquet hall starts to fill up, but there is still room for more guests. So he tells his servant: "Go out to the highways and hedges, and compel people to come in, that my house may be filled" (Lk 14:23). "Compel people to come in," *compelle intrare*: his eagerness went to this extreme.

The command is categorical because the call to salvation is universal. St. Josemaría said,

> *It is not a physical push but an abundance of light, of doctrine. It is the spiritual stimulus of your prayer and work, which bear authentic witness to doctrine. It is all the sacrifices you offer. It is the smile that comes to your lips because you are children of God: your filiation, which imbues you with a serene happiness (although at times your life will also have setbacks), which the others see and envy. Add to this your human bearing and charm, and here we have the content of the* compelle intrare.[16]

Hence it is not a question of forcing anyone; rather it is an ever-new combination of prayer and friendship, witness and generous sacrifice—a joy that is shared, a human warmth that draws others freely.

---

16   St. Josemaría, *Letter*, October 24, 1942, 9; see also St. Josemaría, *Friends of God*, 37.

God acts "by attraction,"[17] reaching souls through the joy and appeal in the life of Christians. Therefore, apostolate is love that overflows. A heart that knows how to love knows how to draw others. *We attract everyone with our heart*, St. Josemaría said. *Therefore I ask that everyone may have a very big heart: if we love souls, we will attract them.*[18] Indeed, nothing attracts as strongly as an authentic love, especially in a day and age when many people have never known the warmth of God's love. True friendship is "the mode of doing apostolate that St. Josemaría found in the Gospel narratives."[19] Philip drew Bartholomew; Andrew brought Peter; and the men who brought the paralytic to Jesus at Capernaum must have been good friends of his.

In a Christian, in a child of God, friendship and charity are one and the same thing. They are a divine light which spreads warmth.[20] Having friends requires diligent personal contact; example and sincere loyalty; the readiness to help others, to mutually assist one another; empathy and listening; the ability to take on others' needs. Friendship is not an instrument for the apostolate; rather apostolate itself is, at heart, friendship: the generous desire to share one's life with others. Of course, we want our friends to draw closer to God, but we are ready to let this happen when and how God wants. Although it's only natural that an apostle wants to see good results

17   Pope Benedict XVI, Homily (May 13 2007); Pope Francis, Homily (May 3, 2018).
18   St. Josemaría, Notes from a Family Get-Together, May 10, 1967, in *Crónica* 1967, p. 605
19   Msgr. Fernando Ocáriz, *Letter*, February 14, 2017, 9.
20   St. Josemaría, *The Forge*, 565

and to be influential with others, we should never forget that the apostles continued following Jesus even when almost everyone else went away (Jn 6:66–69). The results would come with the passage of time (see Acts 2:37–41).

A young fellow once asked St. Josemaría, "Father, what can we do to get many people to 'whistle?'"[21] St. Josemaría answered right away: *A lot of prayer, loyal friendship and respect for freedom.* The young fellow wasn't satisfied, so he said, "But doesn't that mean going too slowly, Father." *No, because the vocation is su-per-na-tu-ral,* he replied, emphasizing each syllable. *A second was enough to turn Saul into Paul. Then, three days of prayer, and he became an ardent apostle of Jesus Christ.*[22]

It is God who calls and the Holy Spirit who moves a person's heart. The apostle's role is to accompany their friends with prayer and sacrifice, not becoming impatient on receiving a no to their suggestions, nor getting angry when someone refuses to be helped. A true friend relies on the other person's strong points to help them grow and tries not to criticize. They know when it is best to keep quiet, and when a different "tack" is needed, not dwelling on the negative but rather striving to draw out the best in each person.

21   In Madrid in the 1930s, "to whistle" was a slang term that meant "to function well." St. Josemaría used it to refer to the fact that someone had asked for admission to Opus Dei. This has now become a family expression in the Work.
22   St. Josemaría, Notes from a Family Get-Together, April 24, 1967, in *Crónica* 1967, p. 506.

Without becoming bothersome, and always with a smile, we can quietly offer polite suggestions, as our Lord did. And we will always keep enkindled in our heart the eager desire that many people may come to know him better. *You and I, children of God, when we see people, we need to see souls: here is a soul, we should say to ourselves, a soul who has to be helped, a soul who needs to be understood, a soul we have to live alongside, a soul who has to be saved.*[23]

---

23   St. Josemaría, Meditation, February 25, 1963, in *Crónica* 1964, IX, p. 69.

CHAPTER 11

TOWARD THE FULLNESS OF LOVE

Paul Muller

C*hrist's way can be summed up in one word: love... we must have a big heart and share the concerns of those around us. We must be able to forgive and understand; we must sacrifice ourselves, with Jesus Christ, for all souls.*[1] "[H]aving loved his own who were in the world, he loved them to the end" (Jn 13:1). These are the words St. John uses in his Gospel to introduce Jesus' surprising gesture before beginning his paschal meal. When they were all seated at the table, Jesus "rose from supper, laid aside his garments, and girded himself with a towel. Then he poured water into a basin, and began to wash the disciples' feet, and to wipe them with the towel with which he was girded" (Jn 13:4–5).

---

1   St. Josemaría, *Christ Is Passing By*, 158.

Jesus washes the apostles' feet: the feet of men who were weak, but chosen to be the foundation of his Church. They had all been afraid amid the storm on the lake; they had doubted the Master's ability to feed a large crowd of people; they had heatedly argued over who would be the greatest in his kingdom. But they had also begun to experience the suffering involved in following him. And they hadn't left him, as so many others did, after his discourse on the Bread of Life in the synagogue at Capernaum. They had accompanied him on his long trips throughout the land of Israel, and they knew that some now wished he were dead.

Peter is astonished when Jesus begins washing their feet. He can't understand it and rebels: "Lord, do you wash my feet?" Jesus replies, "What I am doing you do not know now, but afterward you will understand." But Peter insists, "You shall never wash my feet" (Jn 13:6–8). Simon's forceful reply is surprising. He doesn't mean it as a rejection; rather it is his love for our Lord that leads to his refusal. But Jesus makes clear his mistake: "If I do not wash you, you have no part in me" (Jn 13:8).

You Will Understand Later

Right from his first encounter with the Master, St. Peter had been growing interiorly. Little by little he had begun to understand who Jesus is, the Son of the living God. But our Lord's passion is drawing near, and Peter still has a long way to go. In the Upper Room a scene with two acts takes place: the washing of the apostles' feet and the institution of the Eucharist. And Peter begins to discover the depth of God's love, and how deeply this love challenges him personally. Up to now, the commandment to love one's neighbor as oneself is still mainly words for him and hasn't taken root in his heart as deeply as Jesus wants. And so, he rebels. He refuses to accept that God's will for him is a life of love and humble service to every man and woman, no matter who they are.

Peter's experience can often be repeated in our own life. We too can find it hard to understand what our Lord wants, and we need time to grasp the most basic truths. In our heart a great desire for love can mix with less noble intentions; often we are paralyzed by fear, and the words on our lips are not accompanied by deeds. We love our Lord, and we realize that the divine vocation is our most precious jewel: so much so that we have sold everything to buy it. But the passing of the years, changing circumstances, certain unpleasant situations, or the fatigue of daily work can cloud our path.

It can also be the case that we have not yet attained the degree of human and spiritual maturity required to live our vocation as a path of love. Our charity toward our neighbor can be dragged down by distortions that diminish the mystery of the human person created in God's image: sentimentalism, which leads to a response based on the momentary perception of things rather than a deep relationship with God and our fellow men and women; voluntarism, which results from forgetting that the Christian life means above all letting God love us and love through us; or perfectionism, which sees human deficiencies as somehow foreign to God's plan.

Nevertheless, precisely because God takes into account our personal limitations, he is not surprised nor does he grow tired at seeing us complicate or even disfigure our vocation. He has called us, like Peter, when we were sinners, and he insists, "If I do not wash you, you have no part in me." Simon Peter stops protesting: "Lord, not my feet only but also my hands and my head!" (Jn 13:8–9). Jesus knows that Peter is reacting out of love, and so he replies just as forcefully. The apostle's heart responds with the impetuous ardor we expect from Peter: "not my feet only but also my hands and my head!" Is Peter even aware of the meaning of what he is saying? What happens later that night to him seems to show that he isn't. He will come to understand it later, bit by bit: through the suffering of Jesus' passion and the joy of the Resurrection, thanks to the action of the Holy Spirit. But his dialogue with Jesus teaches us that to reach the fullness of love the first step is to discover Jesus' tender affection for each of us; and to realize that, by rectifying our mistakes and miseries, we will become more and more like him.

Steps toward Freedom

Following Jesus means learning to love as he does. It is an ascending path, and also an arduous one, but at the same time it is a path of freedom. "The freer we are, the more we can love. And love is demanding: 'Love bears all things, believes all things, hopes all things, endures all things' (1 Cor 13:7)."[2] When still a young priest,

---

2   Msgr. Fernando Ocáriz, *Letter*, January 9, 2018, 5.

St. Josemaría discovered this path of ascent toward freedom: *Steps: to be resigned to the will of God; to conform to the will of God; to want the will of God; to love the will of God.*[3]

The lowest step toward freedom is that of resignation. It is the least generous of the four and can easily give way to spiritual lukewarmness. One could describe it as putting up with a situation without growing through it: putting up with it because we have to, accepting "what fate has dealt me." It is true that fortitude, which is a cardinal virtue, also requires putting up with difficulties, offering resistance. But this leads to a growth in freedom, because one grasps and wants the good that makes resistance worthwhile. Resignation, in contrast, fails to grasp any good, or sees it so tenuously that it fails to generate joy. At times, even for a certain length of time, we will be able to last in this situation by making a considerable effort. But when a person takes on a permanent attitude of resignation, sadness will bit by bit worm its way in.

Conforming to God's will is a higher stage. We accept reality and try to conform to it. We shouldn't confuse this conformity with the attitude of a person without ideals, who has no dreams or aspirations to live for. Rather it is the realistic attitude of a person who knows that every good desire is pleasing to God. A person who conforms in this sense learns to enter, bit by bit, into God's way of thinking, with the conviction that everything works for the good of those who love God (Rom 8:28).

3   St. Josemaría, *The Way*, 774.

This process of conforming to God's will is called to rise higher, and we begin to *want* God's will. St. Josemaría prayed: *Lord, help me to be faithful and docile towards you, like clay in the potter's hands. Then it will not be I who live, but you, my Love, who will live and work in me.*[4] Persons and circumstances we haven't chosen become wanted in themselves because we see them as good: We decide "to choose them." "My God, I chose all that Thou willest,"[5] St. Thérèse of Lisieux said. We become certain, with St. Paul, "that neither death, nor life, nor angels, nor principalities, nor things present, nor things to come, nor powers, nor height, nor depth, nor anything else in all creation, will be able to separate us from the love of God in Christ Jesus our Lord" (Rom 8:38–39). We begin to discover, amid an imperfect world, the "something holy" that is hidden in everyday situations,[6] and we see God's image more clearly in those around us.

Drenched in Christ's Blood

The final step on this path of personal growth is that of love. With St. John, we enter into the heart of Christian revelation: "We know and believe the love God has for us" (1 Jn 4:16). After washing his apostles' feet, our Lord tells them why he has done this: "I have given you an example" (Jn 13:15). He is preparing them for his new

---

4   St. Josemaría, *The Forge*, 875. Cf. Jer 18:6: "like the clay in the potter's hand, so are you in my hand."

5   St. Thérèse of Lisieux, *The Story of a Soul*, chap. 1.

6   See St. Josemaría, *Conversations*, 114.

commandment: "that you love one another; even as I have loved you, that you also love one another" (Jn 13:34). They need to learn to love with the greatest love, even to the point of giving their own life for others, as he will do: "For this reason the Father loves me, because I lay down my life, that I may take it again. No one takes it from me, but I lay it down of my own accord" (Jn 10:17–18). Christ's love is marked by self-giving, rising above oneself, lovingly accepting God the Father's will for each of us. This is what loving God's will means: a joyful and creative affirmation that spurs us interiorly to get out of ourselves. It is a decision that, paradoxically, is the only path for finding ourselves: "For whoever would save his life will lose it, and whoever loses his life for my sake will find it" (Mt 16:25).

But this love is not the same as "extreme moral effort," leading to "a new level of humanity."[7] The "newness" of the new commandment "can come only from the gift of communion with Christ, of living in him."[8] Hence, when he reveals the new commandment, our Lord also gives his apostles the Sacrament of Love. The Eucharist henceforth will be at the center of Christian life, not as a theoretical truth but as a vital necessity.[9]

The hand of Christ has snatched us from a wheat field; the sower squeezes the handful of wheat in his wounded palm. The blood of

7   Joseph Ratzinger (Benedict XVI), *Jesus of Nazareth Part Two: Holy Week: From the Entrance into Jerusalem to the Resurrection* (San Francisco: Ignatius, 2011), p. 63.

8   Ratzinger, *Jesus of Nazareth*, p. 64.

9   See St. Josemaría, *Christ is Passing By*, 154.

Christ bathes the seed, soaking it. Then the Lord tosses the wheat to the winds, so that in dying it becomes life and in sinking into the ground it multiplies itself.[10] We are able to give ourselves because our life is soaked in Christ's blood, leading us to die to ourselves and yield an abundant harvest of joy and peace around us. Our participation in the Sacrifice of Jesus and our adoration of his Real Presence in the Eucharist lead directly to love for our neighbor. Therefore, if we *are not faithful to the divine mission of giving ourselves to others, helping them recognize Christ, we will find it very difficult to understand what the Eucharistic Bread is.* And vice versa: *In order to value and love the Holy Eucharist, we must follow Jesus' path. We must be grain; we must die to ourselves and rise with new life and yield an abundant harvest: a hundredfold!*[11]

Eucharistic Consistency

"Jesus is walking in our midst, as he did in Galilee. He walks through our streets, and he quietly stops and looks into our eyes. His call is attractive and intriguing."[12] When we firmly decide to walk at his side, to live in communion with him, our life is filled with light and little by little takes on a true "Eucharistic consistency."[13] The love and companionship that we receive from him enables us to give

---

10   St. Josemaría, *Christ is Passing By*, 3.

11   St. Josemaría, *Christ is Passing By*, 158.

12   Pope Francis, Apostolic Exhortation to Young People *Christus Vivit* (March 25, 2019), 277.

13   Pope Benedict XVI, Apostolic Exhortation on the Eucharist *Sacramentum Caritatis* (February 22, 2007), 83.

ourselves to others as he gave himself. We begin to discover and bit by bit uproot the obstacles that hinder the growth of Christ's charity in our heart: the tendency to do the minimum required in fulfilling our duties; the fear to go too far in our affection and service to others; the lack of understanding when faced with other people's limitations; the pride that demands others recognize our good actions, thus sullying our right intention.

St. Josemaría spoke movingly about the joyful life of those who give themselves to Christ and persevere faithfully in following his call. *This path can be summed up in one word: love. If we are to love, we must have a big heart and share the concerns of those around us. We must be able to forgive and understand; we must sacrifice ourselves, with Jesus Christ, for all souls.*[14] We know this goal far exceeds our own capacities. Therefore, we need to beseech our Lord frequently to give us a heart to the measure of his.

If we love with Christ's heart, we shall learn to serve others and we shall defend the truth clearly, lovingly…. Only by reproducing in ourselves the Life of Christ can we transmit it to others. Only by experiencing the death of the grain of wheat can we work in the heart of the world, transforming it from within, making it fruitful.[15] This is the path of faithfulness that, since it is a path of love, is also a path of happiness.

14   St. Josemaría, *Christ is Passing By*, 158.
15   St. Josemaría, *Christ is Passing By*, 158.

CHAPTER 12

THE FRUIT OF FIDELITY

Pablo Edo

The Book of Psalms begins with a hymn of praise for the fruitful life of the person who strives to be faithful to God and his law, and who resists the pressure of the ungodly: "He is like a tree planted by streams of water, that yields its fruit in its season, and its leaf does not wither. In all that he does, he prospers" (Ps 1:3). It is a teaching found frequently in Sacred Scripture: "A faithful man will abound with blessings" (Prv 28:20); "one who sows righteousness gets a sure reward" (Prv 11:18). All of God's works are fruitful, as are the lives of those who respond to his call. Our Lord told the apostles at the Last Supper, "You did not choose me, but I chose you and appointed you that you should go and bear fruit and that your fruit should abide" (Jn 15:16). The only thing he asks of us is that we remain united to him like branches to the vine, since "[h]e who abides in me, and I in him, he it is that bears much fruit" (Jn 15:5).

Down through the centuries, the saints have had abundant experiences of God's generosity. St. Teresa, for example, wrote: "His Majesty is not wont to offer us too little payment for His lodging if we treat him well."[3] He has promised those who are faithful to him that he will receive them in his kingdom with warm praise: "Well done, good and faithful servant; you have been faithful over a little, I will set you over much; enter into the joy of your master" (Mt 25:21). But God doesn't wait until heaven to reward his children; already in this life he lets them share in his divine joy through many blessings. He fills their life with fruits of holiness and virtue and draws out the best from each person's talents. He helps us not to become discouraged by our own weakness and to trust ever more fully in his strength. Moreover, through his faithful children God also blesses those around them. "By this my Father is glorified, that you bear much fruit" (Jn 15:8).

We are going to consider here some of the fruit produced by our fidelity, both in our own life and in that of others. Hopefully these fruits, and many others that only God knows, will spur us to never stop thanking God for his care and closeness. And thus, we will learn to appreciate his love more and more each day.

3   St. Teresa of Ávila, *The Way of Perfection*, ed. Anthony Uyl (Woodstock, Ontario: Devoted Publishing, 2018), p. 125.

A Heaven within Us

A few days before leaving for heaven, St. Josemaría told a group of his children, *God has wished to deposit a very rich treasure in us…. God Our Lord, with all his greatness, dwells within us. Heaven dwells habitually in our hearts.*[4] Our Lord promised the apostles: "If a man loves me, he will keep my word, and my Father will love him, and we will come to him and make our home with him" (Jn 14:23). This is the principal gift God offers us: his friendship and presence in us.

Each day we can contemplate anew in our prayer the truth of God's presence in us and keep it in our memory. Filled with astonishment and gratitude, we will strive to respond as good children to God's immense affection for us. For our Lord "does not come down from Heaven each day in order to remain in a golden ciborium, but to find another Heaven in which He takes such delight—the Heaven of our soul, created in his image and the living temple of the adorable Trinity."[5] This divine gift alone should make us feel infinitely rewarded, and certain of the joy we give to God by being faithful to him.

When physical or moral tiredness comes, when setbacks and difficulties weigh on us, we need to remind ourselves once again that *if God is dwelling in our soul, everything else, no matter how important it may seem, is accidental and transitory, whereas we, in*

4   Salvador Bernal, *A Profile of Mgr. Escrivá, Founder of Opus Dei* (New York: Scepter, 1977), p. 399.

5   St. Thérèse of Lisieux, *Story of a Soul*, chap. 5.

God, stand permanent and firm.[6] The certainty that God is with me, is in me, and that I am in him (see Jn 6:56), is the source of an interior security and hope that has no human explanation. This conviction leads us to be ever more simple—like children—and gives us a broad and trust-filled outlook, a peaceful and joyful heart. Joy and peace well up from the depths of our soul, as the natural fruit of faithfulness and self-giving. This peace and joy are so important and so effective for evangelization that St. Josemaría beseeched God for this gift each day at Mass, for him and for all his daughters and sons.[7]

We have a heaven within us in order to bring it everywhere: to our home, our workplace, our moments of rest, time spent with our friends. "In our day and age, when a lack of peace is seen so frequently in social life, in the workplace, in family life, it is more necessary than ever that we Christians be, as St. Josemaría said, *'sowers of peace and joy.'*"[8] We know by experience that this peace and joy don't belong to us. Hence, we strive to be aware of God's presence in our hearts, so that he may fill us with his gifts and spread them to those around us. This humble sowing is always effective and can reach far beyond our immediate environment: "Peace in the world perhaps depends more on our personal daily and persevering efforts to smile, to forgive and not take ourselves

6   St. Josemaría, *Friends of God*, 93.
7   Bishop Javier Echevarría, *Memoria del Beato Josemaría Escrivá* (Madrid: Rialp, 2000), p. 229.
8   Msgr. Fernando Ocáriz, *Homily,* May 12, 2017.

too seriously, than on the great negotiations carried out between countries, however important these may be."[9]

A Firm and Merciful Heart

When we allow God's presence to take root and bear fruit in us (which in a certain sense is what fidelity is), we progressively acquire an "inner firmness" that enables us to be patient and gentle when faced with setbacks, unexpected events, situations that bother us, and our own and others' limitations. St. John Vianney said that "our faults are like grains of sand next to the great mountain of God's mercies."[10] This conviction helps us to react as God reacts to our failings—with gentleness and mercy—and not to become upset when we encounter obstacles to our personal plans and preferences. We discover, as St. Josemaría said, that all the events in our day are in some way *vehicles of God's will and should be received with respect and love, with joy and peace.*[11] Thus, little by little, we find it easier to pray, to forgive and find excuses for others, as our Lord did, and we quickly recover our peace, if we should lose it.

At times this effort to foster gentleness and mercy in our heart might seem like cowardice to us when faced with behavior that seems to call for condemnation, or with the malice of those trying to do harm. We should recall then how Jesus rebuked his disciples

9   Msgr. Fernando Ocáriz, *Homily,* May 12, 2017.

10   In G. Bagnard, "El Cura de Ars, apóstol de la misericordia," *Anuario de Historia de la Iglesia* 19 (2010), p. 246.

11   St. Josemaría, *Instruction*, May 1935–September 14, 1950, 48.

when they suggested calling down from heaven punishment on the Samaritans who refused to receive him (Lk 9:55). "The Christian's programme—the programme of the Good Samaritan, the programme of Jesus—is 'a heart which sees.' This heart sees where love is needed and acts accordingly."[12] Our patient mercy, which does not become upset or complain when faced with setbacks, thus becomes balsam with which God heals the contrite of heart, binds up their wounds (Ps 147:3), and makes the path of conversion easier and more attractive for them.

An Effectiveness We Can't Even Imagine

Building up and making known a strong self-image and personal profile is often indispensable today in order to make an "impact" in social media and the working world. Nevertheless, if we lose sight of the reality that we live in God, that he *is calways near us*,[13] this concern can become a subtle obsession to be accepted, to be recognized, "followed," and even admired. We could then experience the constant need to verify the value and importance of everything we do or say.

This eagerness to be recognized by others and to receive tangible verification of our own worth reflects, although in a misguided way, a deep truth. For each of us is of great value—so much so that God has wanted to give his life for each one of us. But we can easily fall

12   Pope Benedict XVI, Encyclical on Christian Love *Deus Caritas Est* (December 25, 2005), 31.

13   St. Josemaría, *The Way*, 267.

into demanding, in quite subtle ways, the love and recognition that we can only receive as a gift. Our Lord said in the Sermon on the Mount: "Beware of practicing your piety before men in order to be seen by them; for then you will have no reward from your Father who is in heaven" (Mt 6:1); and even more radically: "[D]o not let your left hand know what your right hand is doing" (Mt 6:3).

The risk of demanding love instead of receiving it will be less if we foster the conviction that God contemplates even the smallest events in our lives with love—because love is in the details. "If you wish to have spectators for your deeds, here you have them: the angels and archangels, and even the God of the Universe."[14] We then experience the self-esteem that comes from knowing we are always accompanied, and we don't need external proofs in order to trust in the effectiveness of our prayer and life; this is true both when we have attained a certain public fame and when our life passes unnoticed by almost everyone. God's loving look is enough for us, and these words of Jesus that we take personally to heart: "[Y]our Father who sees in secret will reward you (Mt 6:4).

We can learn a lot in this regard from the hidden years Jesus spent in Nazareth. There he spent the greater part of his life on earth. Under the loving eyes of his Father in heaven, of Our Lady and St. Joseph, the Son of God was already carrying out in silence, with an infinite effectiveness, the Redemption of mankind. Few people knew him, but there, in the humble workshop of a craftsman,

14   St. John Chrysostom, *Homilies on Saint Mathew*, 19.2.

God was changing forever the history of all men and women. Our life too can share in the abundant fruit produced by Jesus' life, if we show him to others through our own life, if we let him love with our own heart.

Hidden in each tabernacle, and in the depths of our heart, God continues changing the world. Therefore, our life of self-giving, in union with God and our fellow men and women, takes on through the communion of saints an effectiveness we can't measure or even imagine.

> *You don't know whether you are making progress, nor how much. But what use is such a reckoning to you? What is important is that you should persevere, that your heart should be on fire, that you should see more light and wider horizons; that you should work hard for our intentions, that you should feel them as your own—even though you don't know what they are—and that you should pray for all of them.*"[15]

God is the Same as Always

St. Paul encouraged the first Christians to be faithful, to not be afraid to go against the current, and to work with their eyes set on our Lord: "Therefore, my beloved brethren, be steadfast, immovable, always abounding in the work of the Lord, knowing that in the Lord your labor is not in vain" (1 Cor 15:58). St. Josemaría often echoed this exhortation of the apostle: *If you are faithful you will be*

15   St. Josemaría, *The Forge*, 605.

able to boast of victory, and in your life you will not experience defeat. If we work with an upright intention and the desire to fulfil God's Will, there is no such thing as failure. With success or without it, we have still triumphed because we have worked for Love.[16]

On any vocational path it can happen that, after a period of joyful self-giving, we may feel the temptation to become discouraged. We may think that we haven't been generous enough, or that our faithfulness has yielded scant fruit and little apostolic success. It is good then to recall God's assuring words: "[M]y chosen… shall not labor in vain" (Is 65:22–23). As St. Josemaría said: *To be a saint necessarily entails being effective, even though the saint may not see or be aware of it.*[17] God sometimes allows his faithful ones to undergo trials and hardships in their work, in order to make their soul more beautiful and their heart more tender. When, despite our eagerness to please God, we become discouraged or tired, let us continue working with a "sense of mystery"—realizing that our effectiveness

is often invisible, elusive and unquantifiable. We can know quite well that our lives will be fruitful, without claiming to know how, or where, or when.… No single act of love for God will be lost, no generous effort is meaningless, no painful endurance is wasted.… Let us keep marching

16   St. Josemaría, *Alone with God*, 314.
17   St. Josemaría, *The Forge*, 920.

forward; let us give him everything, allowing him to make our efforts bear fruit in his good time.[18]

Our Lord asks us to work with abandonment and trust in his strength and not in our own, in his vision of the world and not in our limited perception.

As soon as you truly abandon yourself in the Lord, you will know how to be content with whatever happens. You will not lose your peace if your undertakings do not turn out the way you hoped, even if you have put everything into them, and used all the means necessary. For they will have "turned out" the way God wants them to.[19]

The awareness that God can do all things and that he sees and stores up all the good that we do, however small and hidden it may seem, will help us

to be sure and optimistic in the difficult moments that may arise in the history of the world or in our personal life. God is the same as always: all-powerful, all-wise, and merciful. And at every moment he is able to draw good out of evil and great victories out of defeats, for those who trust in him.[20]

---

18   Pope Francis, Apostolic Exhortation on the Proclamation of the Gospel *Evangelii Gaudium* (November 24, 2013), 279.

19   St. Josemaría, *Furrow*, 860.

20   Bishop Javier Echevarría, *Pastoral Letter*, November 4, 2015.

Relying on God's strength, we will live in the middle of the world as his children and become sowers of peace and joy for everyone at our side. This is the patient work that God carries out personally in our hearts. Let us allow him to illumine all our thoughts and inspire all our actions—like Our Lady, who rejoiced to see the great works God was carrying out in her life. May we too say with Mary each day, Fiat!: "[L]et it be to me according to your word" (Lk 1:38).